Sauce Supreme

P. A. Land

Published by Dawn Rite Publishing

www.dawnrite.co.uk

ISBN: 1480105775
ISBN-13: 978-1480105775

DEDICATION

To those who think they know how.

CONTENTS

CHAPTER ONE - INTRODUCTION

The objective of this book is to set down from the managerial viewpoint a series of events that took place from 1979 to 1983. Events offset against a background of political ideology that became known as "privatisation"; events which in fact resulted in the annihilation of one of the finest and oldest hotel companies in the world and concluded a piece of transport history of the United Kingdom. Whether this was desirable or not is for others to decide on the facts. Whether it was done well or if it was a piece of bureaucratic bungling supporting weak politicians; whether the past managerial record laid the path, are matters for others to decide on presentation of the facts. The one thing that is certain is that a world renowned company in the hotel industry was destroyed.

Railway hotels are an integral part of history of both the transportation industry and the lodging industry. The history of the railway hotels has been recorded in several works on the history of the lodging industry and it is sufficient by way of introduction to note that in the development of its transportation business each railway company created an opportunity for its travellers to be accommodated at the end of their journey. The history of those premises is very long and it is claimed that the Midland Hotel, Derby, was the first railway hotel in the world. At the time of development of the railway hotels there was no comparable development on the lines of groups of hotels as we now know them. Each company developed its hotels as an adjunct of its main business. The ultimate format was different. There was initially no sense of deliberate group hotel development.

The business was developed as free enterprise and only one hotel was acquired under public ownership. Nationalisation after the war brought Railway hotels into state ownership and it has been in its attempt to return the hotels to a free enterprise financing base that either government, bureaucracy or management annihilated the business and great traditions of British Transport Hotels.

After the war and with nationalisation of railways, British Transport Commission emerged, one part of which was a hotel executive. This executive was responsible for the administration, functional control and operation of the hotels, railway refreshment rooms and restaurant car services. It was administered from a headquarters in Marylebone Road; the hotels were controlled through a line management reporting to four area superintendents.

Major G. C. Jarrett controlled London and the Southern area from London; Mr.E. R. Cottett controlled the North West and Midlands from Manchester; Mr. J. L. Meadowcroft controlled the Eastern area from York and Mr. W. J. Vachet controlled the Scottish area from Glasgow. The refreshment rooms were controlled by Mr. E. K. Portman-Dixon as Refreshment Room Superintendent and under his control there were 17 districts. Restaurant Cars were controlled by Mr. W. P. Keith and the organisation structure followed the same geographical areas as were covered by the Railway regions.

At that time there were 49 hotels. By any standard, they formed a formidable hotel group, setting very high quality market objectives.

The Hotel Executive itself was headed by Lord Inman as Chairman with Mr Frank Hole the full-time member. Part-time members were Mrs. Gasging, Sir Harry Methven and Mr. Wimble. The executive as a whole and the full-time member in particular assumed responsibility for everything that happened in the course of the management and administration of the business. Group thinking began to emerge and emphasis was laid on a principle that the business was to be run as a single entity and not as a series of independent units working along separate lines. Centralisation of control was clearly considered to be important and those responsible for management were required to see that the hotel and catering service was as efficient as it could be by making the best possible use of staff, materials and equipment placed at their disposal within the policy laid down by the executive. The task of an administration was to provide the facilities and supplies required by management and to keep the management on the right lines so far as policy, standards, finance, industrial relations and general maintenance were concerned.

This organisation policy moved power to a centre. The policy was formulated by a secretary; a chief officer for domestic services, Miss P.M. Oxonford; a chief financial officer, Mr. A. R. D'Amount; a chief officer for personal, Mr. J. G. Norton; a purchasing officer, Mr. E. J. Davis; an officer for wines, spirits and beers, Mr S. Sweeney and a chief works officer, Mr. S. P. Smith. It was inevitable that these administrative officers had to be assisted and slowly Assistants began to emerge in the various areas of activity. Rightly or wrongly, thus emerged a highly centralised and growing organisation on which the development of the Company was based.

In 1962, shortly after the disbandment of British Transport Commission, British Transport Hotels Limited was formed into a company. This created the opportunity to enable the company to develop alongside, if not as a part of, the private sector.

The opportunity was missed because there was no development. There started gentle attrition, political interference, bureaucratic meddling and constraints placed on the business which prevented it developing as its competitors in the private sector were able to develop. It was never allowed to take the opportunities that were presented by the developing tourism market or by the development of air travel. From then onwards, instead of progressing as a virile enterprising body, it began to stagnate as is inevitable in any business that does not have drive from its owners. A great opportunity was lost after 1962. There were good resources, there were good people who were perfectly capable of developing the business if only there had been the will from the owners.

Changes of management endeavoured to correct that position. Studies carried out by Cooper & Lybrand in 1975 pointed towards a greater decentralisation. The possibility of developing the company as part of the National Enterprise Board was considered. There were many advantages in that route since it was a way to escape the dead hand that was put on to British Rail. There was nothing that could be done as part of the National Enterprise Board that could not be done as part of B.R., provided politically B.R. had been encouraged to act like a normal commercial organisation in the handling of its subsidiary companies. Senior management were within an ace of being capable of running the business exactly as any free enterprise business would be run but it was clear that there was a lack of will and a lack of understanding by bureaucracy and politicians as to how a business should be controlled and the role its shareholders should play if it were to live in the private sector. It was not the only business that was under public ownership, living in a highly competitive market where its competitors did not have the dead hand of bureaucracy and politics upon them. One need look no further than the road industry.

During 1977, the British Railways Board reviewed their position and began to form their views on their policy for their hotel and catering subsidiary. The Board, in January 1977, had considered submissions on the business objectives and were anxious to take the necessary action to give their subsidiary businesses the maximum freedom consistent with overall interest of the Board. Attempts were made with the Department of Transport to identify the issues requiring action by Government and those where the Board could take action itself. In order to make progress quickly, an interim reorganisation of the Hotels Company began to be implemented in 1978. At that time the Hotels Company was divided into a Hotels Division and a Travellers-Fare Division, each of which was planned to continue with its own Divisional Board and its own Managing Director.

A new British Transport Hotels Board would take responsibility for overseeing the two divisions and also for the provision of certain common services. There was no plan for each Division to develop as a separate company and it was intended that British Transport Hotels should remain as the statutory operating company. The Divisional Boards were required to produce their action plan to progress the areas of development of their own businesses to endeavour to look into a five year future and, in the case of the Travellers-Fare Division, to have regard to its future relationship with the rail passenger business.

The Railways Board intended to do something generally about its subsidiaries and endeavour to create in them the same disciplines and opportunities as were enjoyed by their competitors in the private sector. This made people think about where they might be capable of taking the company. Initial changes were not intended as a long term organisation structure, but as an interim measure to start moves in the general direction of the change, with the longer term structure emerging as soon as possible.

Many new ideas were now being brought to the force and openly discussed, such as:-

1. To set up joint companies with private concerns or other nationalised transport undertakings, like British Airways;

2. To acquire leasing or management contracts of hotels both in the UK and abroad;

3. To rationalise the portfolio of properties by disposing of those that were clearly not going to be profitable and reinvesting the proceeds in other profitable enterprises;

4. To expand the retail facilities at stations with an eye in the longer term to developing a station into a large retail complex;

5. To take over those BR owned public houses which were let to individuals or companies as current leases expired;

6. To introduce a contract arrangement for the provision of catering or trains.

A great new dawn appeared early in 1978 with a Board clear in its intent to set up British Transport Hotels Limited as a company with appropriate freedoms to enable it to develop alongside competitors.

On 17th March 1978, the British Railways Board agreed the terms of reference for BTH which it saw as simply the first step towards achieving the objectives sought by the British Railways Board.

Continuing to move with speed and determination, the BR Board announced the reorganising or British Transport Hotels on 21st April 1978 as part of the corporate strategy of British Rail for the more successful development of its subsidiary businesses to generate the confidence of the Government, as shareholder and banker, and also that of the customer. It indicated the importance of its hotel business being increasingly successful in the international tourist industry and of rail catering, where the part played by catering in attracting customers to rail travel was seen as an expanding role in the future.

In order to preserve and develop links with rail business, Mr. R G Reid, then Marketing Member of British Railways Board and a career railway man became Chairman of the Travellers-Fare Divisional Board. Sir Alexander Glen, former Chairman of the British Tourist Authority, became Chairman of the Hotels Division Board and Mr. R. L. E. Lawrence, Vice Chairman of British Railways remains Chairman of British Transport Hotels Board with Sir Alexander Glen as his Deputy. The BTH Board also included Miss Prudence Leith, an acknowledged international figure in the catering business and Mr. James Forbes, a Vice Chairman of Tate & Lyle, a former Finance Director of Cadbury Schweppes, a Member of the Council of the Institute of Chartered Accountants for England and Wales and a man held in highest esteem in the city. There was thus established a strong non executive Board membership to direct this business enterprise.

It remained to make one key appointment, that of a Chief Executive to implement the plans of the BTH Board. In July 1978, the author joined British Transport Hotels Limited as Group Managing Director. This key appointment was considered best filled by a person of proven business administrative ability rather than by a product man. I had a background in business as a Chartered Accountant where I had been at the top of my profession in the private sector before joining British Rail in 1963 to help with the great changes that were made in the Beeching era. I gained intensive experience in helping to implement the 1968 Transport Act where I had taken the leading role in creating National Carriers Limited from the very diverse road transport operations of the railways and moved that company into the National Freight Corporation in 1969.

The Board was completed by three executive directors, namely Mr. Ian Jack and Mr. Bill Currie with extensive product knowledge and Mr John Tee who led the finance operation.

Thus the stage was set. A Parent Board where it wished its subsidiary to go, a Company Board of Directors well experienced in the particular business and in business generally.

CHAPTER TWO – THE PLAN CREATED IN 1979

Some idea of the size of the business for which a plan for development had to be devised can be obtained from the following:-

• 29 hotels in England and Scotland, one being 5-star and the remainder all broadly described as in the upper market.

• Six eighteen-hole golf courses and two nine-hole golf courses.

• 980 catering services per day being provided on trains, comprising 520 full meal/hot snack services and 460 cold buffet services.

• On station premises – 390 retail and catering outlets were operating including restaurants, buffets, kiosks, off-licences, supermarkets, newsagents and pubs together with 1,200 vending machines.

• Cellars handling 1.2 million bottles of wine per annum.

• Three laundries dealing with 22 million items of laundry per annum.

• Capital expenditure programmes of £5 million per annum.

• Over 10,000 employees.

• Turnover of £100 million per annum.

By any standards this was a large, diverse business and acknowledged internationally in hotel, catering and tourism business.

The plan that was created envisaged the profitable exploitation of the Company's strengths to meet identified market needs by repositioning resources and changing administration to speed up decision making. The BTH Board completed its work in the first months of 1979 and submitted its proposals to British Railways Board in May of that year.

The Plan proposed an integrated company consisting of a group of eight fully accountable businesses and attendant organisation structure. This was seen as an evolution from the sharper distinction that had been drawn between hotels and the two Travellers Fare activities of the retail and catering and train catering. The commitment to the railway passenger business was protected by the provision of a catering product according the requirements laid down by the passenger business management. Whilst the Company took the initiative in suggesting the kind of services that should be provided, it was the decision of the railway passenger management as to what those services would be, having due regard to their business objectives. In respect of retail and catering, our objective was to encourage railway operators to take more account of the fact that at many main line terminals, particularly in the main major cities the customers of the retail and catering business outlets at the stations were not confined to people holding a train ticket. In respect of train catering and price structure within which the product was to be controlled was also subject to the approval of the rail operators.

Each of the eight businesses was seen as being capable of independent development within a family where the benefits of being part of a larger entity would be used to advantage.

The Company was determined to reduce the level of overheads but nevertheless it had to remember that it was a subsidiary of the Railways Board administration and it could not behave wholly in the manner of responding to private sector owners. The requirements that the bureaucracy placed on the Railways Board have to be reflected into its subsidiaries. But, in principle, what the Company decided to do was to identify separately the items of overhead that were needed in its opinion to run business, and those overheads were then charged to the part of the organisation using them. At the same time it was determined to decentralise its activities to ensure that more and more of the overheads were not being incurred by the central organisation (that was affectionately known as the Kremlin at St Pancras Chambers) for its own sake but by the people who were actually running the businesses close to the ground. Overheads had to be made part of the profit and loss account management of the line managers. It is remarkable how overheads that are considered unnecessary and a useless drag when "they" at a centre incur them and then allocate, suddenly become a vital expense in a decentralised unit!

There was no financial structure to which the BTH Board could respond. The Company was being properly accounted for and there was a balance sheet which gave an indication of the value of the capital investment in terms of historic written down figures. Opinions had been expressed from time to time about the market value of the properties as assets and about its value on an ongoing concern basis. It is imperative in any organisation that performance and accountability are not judged against moving targets and the BTH Board set about endeavouring to establish in its plan a financial structure against which it could be judged and on one where the Board would be able to stand proud when they had met their financial objective as had been agreed. There was no point whatsoever in continuing on a basis of not knowing how much profit was acceptable and being tied to a capital investment programme that related to the problems of the railway and its borrowing limit. The Company had to have a proper structure against which profit performance could be judged as it responded to the changing market situations in which it had to live. National borrowing targets and railway capital investment programmes actually have nothing to do with running a hotel business. My past experience did not give me much hope that the Civil Service bureaucracy would comprehend that fact.

In order to draw some conclusion for the short term, the Company suggested that its financial objective should be based on financial self-sufficiency rather than a target return on capital employed. Accordingly, it based its plan on a primary Company financial objective to generate sufficient cash from its operations to provide for replacement of resources (except for buildings), minor development and remuneration of capital investment.

Minor development implied projects designed to enhance or modestly extend the existing product, such projects frequently being defensive in the sense of protecting current business and in practice a certain overlap with resource replacement expenditure was seen as inevitable. Major investment was defined as new facilities on a significant scale, which usually meant increasing capacity to earn. The funding of these would not be exclusively from trading cash flow but from new investment from outside sources, or by realisation of assets which, in the Board's view, were incapable of trading profitably.

The key first objective of the Board would be thus achieved, that of being financially independent of the problems of financing the Railways.

By reference to the Company's track record, its product performances and an objective assessment of the strengths and weaknesses, the eight separate accountable business sectors were identified:-

• Leisure Hotels – 11 hotels were placed in the category and included Gleneagles, Turnberrry, Stratford, York, Mortonhampstead and both Edinburgh hotels.

• City Hotels – 12 hotels were placed in this category, the five in London and provincial hotels such as Manchester, Leeds and the two in Glasgow.

• Investment Hotels – 6 hotels were identified which for reasons of their size or the locality they served, did not appear to be compatible with those selected for the Leisure or City sectors. Contrary to the belief of many of the staff at the time, these were not six hotels singled out for sale but there were singled out to be freed from the group image or any idea of a common BTH standard. The whole intention was that there were to be developed individually or associated with another operator for the development in a totally different operation. On the other hand, it was always accepted that if the environment in which they were situated improved and it appeared sensible to invest in them, this would be done and they would then be moved into one of the other two divisions.

• Retail & Catering – Contrary to its common music hall image, this activity is not based on selling old pork pies to people about to miss a train. Over a number of years all the skills of modern merchandising had been brought to bear on this business and the slow process to eliminate its old image was being achieved. Fundamentally this Division was seen as retailing business. There were exceptions when reasonably sophisticated restaurants were being operated and where food was being prepared on the premises, but in the generality of things, we saw ourselves dealing with a retailing operation over a very wide range of products. Already, the Division was operating off-licences, small supermarkets, pubs, kiosks, newsagents. It was tedious to see business operations allowed on the station premises provided they were privately owned when the Division was not allowed to carry out the same operations because they were publicly owned. Furthermore, the law prevented the Division trading in the high street even when they had produced a good and profitable operation on the station concourse.

• Train Catering – This mobile retail and catering operation is a specialist management style. Basically its merchandise is the same as that provided on station establishments though, for obvious reasons, its scope has to be much smaller. It also has a limitation to a market comprising those actually travelling on a train and that limitation alone makes it a not viable enterprise measured in strict commercial terms. Over the years, a great deal of nonsense has been written and said out of mischief or ignorance about the service quality and expectation. A complete rethink was necessary but any change must avoid being labelled as copying the airlines. One thing is certain, no restaurant in the world would run a business in a high street based on the great English breakfast and kippers on the Brighton line nor would it have to tolerate the fuss created by complaints via M.P.'s from their constituents or the M.P.'s themselves if the steak and kidney was not like that made by their mothers.

• Wines – A thriving business had been built up over the years based on the Company's very high reputation for good wines. The Malmaison Wine Club was well established and opportunity was seen for the development of the wholesale business and, in due time and within the limitations of the law, the development of retail high street businesses.

• Technical Services – Over recent years, the size of the Technical Services ability of the Company had been diminished but it was still substantial in numbers and very great in experience. It appeared obvious to set this division up as a separate business, encouraging it to seek outside commissions. At the same time, it was felt desirable to remove from the hotels and catering divisions the burden of having to use an internal technical service for the whole of their developments. The opportunity was created to take the broadest view on style and design and use all concepts of the modern technology and materials.

• Linen Hire – the Company had substantial laundry and dry cleaning activities in three centres of the country. It also had a very large contract for the provision of laundry services to Railways for seat covers, sleeping car linen, etc. Whilst the facilities at its disposal were working to rather less than half capacity, there was considerable opportunity available to seek outside commercial opportunities, but, here again, the law that prevented such development had to be overcome and refurbishment and renewal of plant was very necessary.

In addition, the Board saw new opportunities associated with its main stream business that could include travel agencies, booking agencies, car hire services, tour operations and the like.

To be successful, a complete review of the organisation structure had to be made and each of the eight businesses was placed under the control of a Chief Executive who was given maximum autonomy. Corporate functions were reduced to four, namely Finance, Personnel, Legal and Supplies. These were functional and not line command. The function, whilst directed on a Company basis, would be undertaken under the line command of the Chief Executive of each division. Thus the Group Managing Director controlled the Company through approximately twelve senior people, being eight Chief Executives and four functional heads.

Each Chief Executive was supported by a Divisional Board and it was an objective to achieve a position where the Chief Executive was Chairman of his Divisional Board. At this stage, the Board planned to introduce a further unusual piece of organisation thinking which was to invite non executive Board Members to become Members of Divisional Boards, sitting under the Chairmanship of the Chief Executive of the Division. The objective of this was to make the Chief Executive think more and more about the business he was running whilst encouraging others to achieve the product objectives.

In the Leisure Hotels Division, the Board saw the greatest potential growth of demand which would arise both from tourists and from the business sector in respect of conferences and incentive travel. The facilities of the hotels in the Leisure Division and the locations in important tourist centres were seen as particular advantages. A capital investment programme provided for the provision of private bathrooms to every room and such major developments as leisure and conference facilities at Gleneagles; a conference and sports complex at Turnberry; a new 18hole golf course, clubhouse and conference facilities at the Welcome at Stratford on Avon; refurbishment of the Caledonian in Edinburgh; and at York the building of a new hotel on some former railway property that was designed to handle the growing coach tour business. The plan envisaged a total expenditure of £7 million over five years.

In the City Hotels Division, it was thought that the slow growth of UK economy might adversely affect hotels in areas that were mainly serving business communities. The Company's existing City Hotels with the advantage of improved intercity travel by road and rail would continue to satisfy an on-going need for good quality accommodation and business facilities in provincial city centres. It was not envisaged that there should be any extension of the capacity of existing resources. Major investment proposals were included to provide a complete change in the catering arrangements at the Great Western Royal Hotel; redevelopment of the kitchen at the Great Eastern; the refurbishment of the Grosvenor and a development of La Fourchette Restaurant in the Central, Glasgow. The total investment proposed for the first five years was 8.7 million.

The six hotels that were placed in the Investment Hotels Division were, without a doubt, problems but they were not put in that Division for the express purpose of being sold. The Investment Hotels was devised to manage properties that were not capable of meeting the same market objectives as those in the Leisure or City Divisions. The problems in each hotel in the Division had sometimes arisen because of increased competition, sometimes because of rebuilding and road layout within a city or because the general commercial life of a city had changed, if not actually disappeared. The Investment Division was always seen as a place where there would have to be radical change or disposal. It was in that order that the management of the Investment Division were told to conduct their business. Hotels which were sufficiently well located to compete with other hotels in the immediate vicinity could be developed provided there was a clear market need. But, when plans could not be made to achieve that, then the best option for disposal, either outright or for joining in partnership with another operator, was to be devised. Over the five years, it was anticipated that rather more than £1 million would be the yield from disposals and, at the same time, a total investment of £1 million was planned for that Division.

The market for the Retail & Catering Division was seen as expanding in the popular catering field based on the fast food concepts where it was considered that there would be considerable growth for about five years but at the same time emphasising the need for improvement of quality standard. Prices were forecast to be very keen and it was believed that profits would arise from high volume rather than from high margins. The Division had made a very successful entry into retailing in small supermarkets, off licences, newspapers and stationery, confectionery and the like. Many opportunities were still to be exploited within a philosophy of a railway station becoming a major retail trading centre to which people could be attracted for reasons other than a need to catch a train. The limiting by statute of the operation to railway premises was resented and considered to be a completely unreasonable constraint to be placed on the business. All investment could be provided out of current earnings. The premises were on short leases from BR and the main investment need was confined to equipment and stock. Whilst the total investment plan of £5 ½ million was envisaged for five years, no provision was made for new retailing operations or for the development into outside catering for which this Division was eminently suited. This was because the Board did not want to have its plans ridiculed as being too expansive until a way could be found to remove the legal constraints on locations for the new business.

The Train Catering Division provided an essential service to the railway passenger business and, as such, its product must be prescribed by that customer. Three levels of service were envisaged, a restaurant car service together with a buffet service; a buffet service where the buffet vehicle is permanently in the train set; and trolley service where there is no catering vehicle on the train. Over many years, the train catering activity had never had the clarity of product requirement that was necessary to give the management an appropriate accountability. It was therefore decided that this Division would move as quickly as possible to establish a contractual arrangement with the Passenger Department of BR for the provision of its service. Such an arrangement had to provide a profit incentive for both parties and leave no doubt in anyone's mind that the product definition was the responsibility of the passenger train management. This is a service which, to all intents and purposes, has no capital investment requirements. Subject to establishing proper contractual arrangements, it was therefore a very important cash contributor to the Company. Whilst this service has been the butt of public abuse, usually from people who don't actually travel on trains, it was not seen in that light at all by the Company management. Here was a product with exciting opportunities for change and the case for change was being spelled out by a team of young managers. Rail passenger management was responding but slowly through its Committee system. Regional rivalry and the reluctance of lower managers to risk pressing for a decision that was too radical for their elders, tended to contribute to slow progress. Lower Railway Managers serve in a highly disciplined product that does not call for the entrepreneurial flair that was necessary in buying their catering requirements.

By 1979, the consumption of wine in the UK had trebled over the previous 18 years but was still far short of the per capita consumption in other countries of Western Europe. Consumption in the UK was forecast to continue to grow at an increasing rate and opportunities were thus seen to develop the business in fine vintage wine which British Transport Hotels and its predecessors had a very high reputation. The Malmaison Wine Club was well established with an excellent reputation for fine wine offering good value for money. The plan was to expand, under strict control, the number and range of the Company's outlets. These outlets were seen to be first the Malmaison Wine Club Mail Order business where competition is from small usually privately owned business and second, the development of Malmaison retail shops where two or three fine wine shops would be established in the more affluent areas and where the Malmaison reputation could successfully compete for a share of the anticipated growth in fine wine consumption. Some off licences had already been developed by the Retail and Catering Division and any further development would be undertaken by that Division with close association with the Wines Division, arranging supplies, influencing sales policy and, where necessary, providing the appropriate expertise. Significant market opportunity was believed to exist in the wholesale side of the business where sales direct to trade were planned to be developed and where the market would be other hotels, restaurants, clubs, directors' dining rooms and small wine businesses. A further opportunity was to be investigated which would enable Malmaison to act as an agent on commission for principals in the wine growing areas. Development of the wine business demanded substantial investment in stock and also acquisition of more suitable cellar premises with good distribution facility. In this developing business no major contribution to cash flow was anticipated for the first two years but when the new markets had been successfully developed, the profits and cash flow looked good. The business had reached a stage where go or get out were the options and we certainly saw ourselves able to match any competition.

Already the Technical Services activity in the Company had been substantially reduced. Many years earlier, the services of architects, surveyors, quantity surveyors, designers, project managers and the like had been exclusively provided from an in-house service. There was no doubting the professional competence and the wide experience of the people who were employed but the Board believed that the Company would be better served if managers were to have the opportunity of other influences. The first move strategically, therefore, would be to reduce the in-house Technical Services to provide for no more than 60% of the budgeted work programme with outside consultants being appointed to meet the balance of the demand. The Board had to remember in planning along these lines that some of its managers felt heavily protected by the established in-house service and, whilst they were eager to criticise the Works Department, they did, in fact, rely on it far too much so that a move requiring them to put something like half their work to outside consultants produced an additional burden for them while pulling the business round to a more appropriate level of profit. The Operating Divisions of the Company would have first call on the services of the Technical Services Division but it was the intention that the Division would set itself up as a normal professional practise, earning a major part of its revenue by working for outside clients. The Board was satisfied with a break-even position in this Division on the basis of in-house work being charged at about 75% of the normal professional scale fees with any services to outside clients at the full scale. After two years, when the Division had established itself, the position would be reviewed.

Since the early 1960's there has been a steady reduction in the number of commercial laundries in the UK. Continuing cost inflation and declining demand resulting from the move away from commercial laundries towards domestic washing machines and launderettes had reduced the overall number of operators. The Company had spare capacity available since its plants were in the main operating on a single day shift basis. Thus, with spare capacity and frustrated customers in hotels, hospitals and restaurants, the Company saw an opportunity for profitable expansion. Further encouragement in the direction came from the fairly recent development of linen hire services which was attractive to many customers as it avoided the expense of capital investment in linen and clothing. The lack of care with which the Company's staff handled our stock of linen had, over a number of years, given cause for concern and it was felt that the opportunity should be taken to move the entire hotel, retail and catering operations into a linen hire basis using the new linen hire division as the owner of the linen. Past investment in equipment had been deplorably low and, to support not only the planned development but the actual existing throughput, a modernisation programme was essential. The Company was faced with a major rebuilding problem at its London laundry and capital expenditure approaching £2 million was envisaged to increase the capacity, improve the efficiency and create more acceptable working conditions. By charging rates which were to be no greater than those that could be provided by outside operations, the division was scheduled to make a significant contribution to the cash flow of the business.

A plan so complete and commending so much change naturally took some little time to be approved by British Railways Board. They were faced with the problem of having a comprehensive response to their request to their subsidiary Board to prepare a Business Plan. It was encouraging when, in its corporate review of the subsidiary companies, BR Board noted that the plan "provides an encouraging prospectus for the future development of the business and as such represents a major step forward. It shows prospects for potential increases in profitability and gives indications of positive development opportunities. On this basis therefore the plan provided a satisfactory contribution for inclusion in the corporate review." That is satisfactorily encouraging but what was at the time a tiny sting in the tail appeared in the words, "this will not necessarily imply acceptance of all the proposed changes; in particular the P.S.O. implications must be kept under review." For the first time in what was subsequently to prove to be a long saga, the BTH saw the indication that they were not actually responding to a body who was master of its destiny, and to whom they may not be able to look for the positive thinking that a subsidiary is entitled to expect from its parent.

The time was now May 1979. An election was in prospect and the Company found itself sometimes alone and sometimes supporting BR people in discussions at the Department of Transport regarding the future developments. Meetings went through the customary agonies of civil servants wanting more information and paper to cover their clear lack of comprehension of either the nature of the business itself or the environment in which it worked in competition with the private sector. Discussion degenerated, concentrating on explaining the projections of volume and profit growth. Details of the sources of revenue and costs were refined, the merit of assessing a heavily front loaded investment programme against the business's medium and long term aims was introduced and explanation of the relationship between train catering and the railway passenger business and the thinking behind the contractual basis for such arrangements was made. More detail on the sources of revenue and cost for station catering together with geographical and functional split was sought. It was noted that it might be helpful to expand on the inter actions with private sector station catering concerns and on the business intentions to take over any major tenancies. The whole effort became the kind of case study we all pass through as students. The civil servants were the masters, they had the power and the management had no option but to live through hours of agonising examination which demanded great patience and calmness because to lose either was immediate failure. We were discovering, but not realising at the time, how easy it was to get the decision "no", a matter which was to play a very important part in discussions that were to take place in a few years' time.

It is difficult to explain the effect of this dead hand of bureaucracy. In the first months of 1979, the new Board had breathed fresh life into the Company. Its proposals had been accepted by its parent Board but now, neither alone nor with BR, could it overcome the final hurdle.

By July, a stalemate had been reached where every question the civil servants could think of had been fully answered but still there was not a "yes" decision to support the British Railways Board's blessing of our plan and, as the department of Transport noted at the time, it was useful to record "our impressions of the points which came out of the discussions. As on previous occasions and with other businesses the intention is to log up points which seem to us worth feeding into the next planning cycle". We seemed to be moving into a position where we had finished one planning cycle without actually reaching a decision except that of deciding what points should be fed into the next planning cycle. The first concerned the general question of the extent of the commentary, where the Department felt that the plan lacked sufficient commentary to enable them to make reasoned judgement on the robustness of the features which it presented. "The papers which were distributed are of help in giving an indication of the considerations which underlie the figures. Nevertheless I hope that next year's plan might incorporate some account of the broad assumptions underlying projected developments in the main areas. I appreciate that it might be difficult in such a disparate business as BTH to make meaningful generalisations." The comments go on to emphasise that they would not wish to see in the plan details of the figures on which the forecast had been based and hoped that the next year's plan would incorporate a fuller assessment of the risk factors affecting all the sectors of the business.

It is a little less than a gross insult to set up a management team as strong as those people who constitute the British Railways Board, for them to appoint a management team with the experience and business knowledge of that that constituted the British Transport Hotels Board and then for the plan that those two bodies have approved to be crawled over by civil servants with such demonstrable lack of business acumen and total disregard for the fact that they were, in their masterly inactivity, constructing to the demise of a company of over 10,000 people.

There must be a better way.

CHAPTER THREE – IMPLEMENTING THE ORGANISATION STRUCTURE

The British Transport Hotels Board found itself with the problem of having to run a business with no decision by the Department as to whether its agreed plan was to be implemented. No business can just stand still; any attempt to do so would be to abandon its responsibilities to the employees and the owners and permit the company to degenerate. At its July 1979 meeting, the BTH Board agreed its organisation structure for submission for the approval of the August meeting of the British Railways Board and, whilst by 2nd August 1979 the British Railways Board had approved the BTH Board proposals, it was not achieved without overcoming one or two problems.

There were a number of different opinions concerning titles which, at the time, seemed to cause a great deal of emotion but, so far as those who were concerned with actually wanting to do the job, were of little importance. I have long come to the conclusion that from all line management structures, we should delete the word "Chief" and the word "Director" simply to eliminate the ridiculous argument which goes on in every piece of organisation as to whether a Chief of something is bigger than a Director of something; whether a Director of a parent Board should be identified as something different, except by law, from a Director of a subsidiary Board; and whether there can be more than one Chief Executive in a business. Of course, we all know exactly what people are really thinking about. They are more concerned with personal ego trips than with clear definition of responsibility. The ego trip concerns what other people will think about the title and the dignity of the individual when it is seen in cold print by friends, enemies and neighbours and, since in most large organisations there is a pecking order for perks, whether one description will attract a wall to wall carpet or a simple foam-backed square (and that's before one even enters the arguments about the colour, make and size of motor-car).

The BTH Board's conclusion was that each division should have a Chief Executive and that he should respond to a divisional board. The Board members were very willing to accept the proposition that they should serve on Divisional Boards and the ultimate objective of the Divisional Board chairman being the Chief Executive. As time went by they made great contributions in that role to the development of the divisional businesses and its senior executives. It was inevitable that they would because we were fortunate in having the right kind of people who saw their role as helping develop the business and its people rather than resting on their dignity as "Directors". Not only did they make a real contribution to the businesses and the personal development of senior people in the division but they so clearly derived pleasure and deep understanding from participating in that way.

While there was ready acceptance of the splitting of the hotels side into three divisions, there was reluctance to set up separate Rail Catering and Retail & Catering Divisions each with its own Chief Executive. The earlier interim organisation had created a separate Travellers Fare Board for that part of its organisation. In a short space of time it was seen within railway circles by railwaymen as a power base from which they were reluctant to be moved. To be Chairman of a Board or to be a Board Member was very important; a power base to influence career thinking more than consideration for the long term development of the company as a whole. On the other hand, it must be remembered that Government had changed and, whilst there was an ideology appearing that saw the need to move hotels into the private sector, this was less certain in the case of the Travellers Fare side of the business. The BTH organisation saw a development of the Retail & Catering Division as a natural for the injection of private sector money as part of its philosophy of the trading complex of a station. While ever that Division could be brigaded with the Train Catering Division which no-one with any knowledge of the product requirement can ever see being financed on a normal private sector basis, a defence was seen for the whole of the Travellers-Fare business by people who were less keen to see private sector involvement. Power in some railway minds is seen by the breadth of command and it is with great reluctance those minds will be forced to give up the size of command. An unfortunate compromise had to be accepted which prevented Jack Simpson and David Bailey coming through in a Divisional Chief Executive role with their own command. The compromise also weakened my overall command since it prevented me from moving Bill Currie away from railway thinking and to give him much greater scope as the second in command of the whole business.

On 2nd August 1979 the British Railways Board agreed the proposals for the reorganisation. In approving the document, they made several very constructive observations. They were able to take a different view on the creation of the Divisional Boards and pointed out that the change must be implemented with care to ensure that another layer of organisation was not being introduced. They particularly wanted to see the Divisional line of command headed by the title Executive Director (this was the final agreed title against that proposed of Chief Executive) responding to the Group Managing Director who reported to the Company Board. They wished care to be taken in any publicity to avoid the impression of a larger bureaucracy being set up when the objective was the reduction of overheads. Similar concern as had been expressed at the Hotels Board was made regarding the wide range of command in geographical terms that was being given to each Executive Director but they accepted that the proposal supported the marketing objective and that the aim of decentralisation of command to each hotel unit was such an important cornerstone of the thinking. There was only one area in which they were a little less strong in support and that was the matter concerning the arrangements for Travellers-Fare. Here they hesitated and required a further submission to be made after consultation with rail management in regard to the future arrangements for Travellers-Fare when relationships being divisions had been clarified. That unfortunately was the kiss of death on progress; it is the equivalent of a poor kick for touch and still left a power base for railwaymen in the continuing Travellers-Fare Board. However, it was nothing about which a fuss was justified. The Board of the Company had obtained adequate support for most of its proposals from its parent Board it, therefore, moved forward with the confidence of that backing.

The subsequent implementation of the organisation involved the detailed consultation procedures with the Trade Unions, all of which serve a very valuable purpose if properly used in making management absolutely convinced about what it is they are going to do. The biggest problem the Board had to face in practice was that of putting the appropriate names into the boxes on the organisation chart and, whilst compromise sometimes had to be made, on the whole the Board were satisfied that in every appointment they made, the man was able or capable of becoming able to do the job. In any change in organisation structure, that of itself is a good start.

CHAPTER FOUR – THE FINANCIAL STRUCTURE

Whilst the Company plan set a financial objective for the future which was related to cash flow, it still left the Board open to criticism as to what the level of profit should be. In normal circumstances it is important for a Board to know what will satisfy its shareholders. The shareholders, British Rail, are influenced by the politicians and both are influenced by a bureaucracy living close to fear of the Treasury. I never had the opportunity of deciding if Politicians had a view. At this time, every civil servant with a real future became expert in the current 'in' thing known as the three R's – recommended rate of return. The fact that no-one could really decide what the recommended rate was and on what it should be judged did not seem to deter enthusiasm for the policy and the Department recorded at that time that they "attached considerable importance to a financial target for the business and that it was agreed that a target should be set for BTH." They were set on a return against a valuation of capital employed in the business and, for our part, we were trying to make them see that the real value of the business might actually have more regard to its ability to earn, and that only when you really were facing up to the option of total disposal on a site value basis did the valuation of properties on an open market matter. Since over 50% of the income came from properties that were integral parts of railway stations or actual railway trains, it was rather difficult to think in terms of a total property disposable value as a base against which to assess capital employed. All of this had been most carefully thought through and considered by the Board before it reached its decision as to financial objective. The Company had to be given a fresh start and a capital structure built up that had some regard to earning ability. It is imperative for any organisation to accept its obligations to reward the capital investment. If possible, it is desirable to set up a means of calculating that reward that gives flexibility to the Company to have different rates or methods or remunerating new investment as opposed to that used for remunerating original investment. The Company proposed the following rules on which a capital structure was to be founded:-

1.   That major new investment would be financed on the basis of cumulative preference shares of 10% issued to the BR Board.

2.   That dividend distribution should be one-third of the profit after interest on any short-term financing. Short-term financing would be used to finance major projects up to the point of establishing the cumulative preference share.

3.   The priority in the use of the cash available for distribution would be:-

(a)   pay interest on short-term borrowing;

(b)   repay short-term loans;

(c)   pay cumulative preference dividends;

(d)   pay equity dividend.

The lines of communication already established with the BR Finance Member had established his support for this type of approach and, by September 1979, the BTH Board had endorsed a proposed financial structure for submission to the BR Board. This submission was approved by the BR Board for implementation. From 1st January 1980.

This was an enormous step forward and one which put the BR Board in a proper financial relationship with its subsidiary. Success or failure could be judged in a commercial way, removing from BTH once and for all the ties with Railway problems of borrowing limited, deficit financing, cash limits and other Treasury gymnastics.

An opening capital structure of £30 million was envisaged of which a quarter should be in the form of 10% loan stock with a fixed redemption period and the remainder as a BR equity. This gave a 3.3: 1 gearing which was felt to be in line with the rest of the industry. A 10% loan stock interest was proposed because that reflected the likely average rate of interest due to the Secretary of State at 31st December 1979. It was proposed that there should be a facility to re-financing the loan stock within five years of the date of redemption.

It was agreed that funds for major development so far as they could not be provided from earnings and from realisations would be provided by a redeemable loan stock issued at the current NLF borrowing rate with a fixed redemption period but which, at the Company's discretion, could be redeemed earlier. The priority in the use of cash was agreed:-

1. Pay interest on short term borrowing.

2. Pay interest on redeemable loan stock.

3. Pay interest on the 10% loan stock.

4. Repay short term borrowing.

One-third of the profit after interest would thereafter accumulate for the BR equity shares for distribution as cash became available.

Provided the profit plan was achieved, the short-term borrowing requirement would be eliminated by 1981/82. The interest on loan stock and redeemable loan stock would be paid in the years in which it was incurred and, by 1982/83, the accrued equity dividend would be paid in full. The value of the equity would have increased by over 50% over the five years excluding any adjustment for revision in capital value of assets.

After about a year as a team, the Company was set to enter 1980 with a plan approved by its parent Board; with a new organisation structure capable of implementing that plan and a financial structure that would enable it to react quickly as any other private sector company would in changing circumstances and trading conditions.

A new Government had come to power with plans to introduce private sector money. The Company were well prepared to take advantage of this philosophy provided, of course, it could continue to take decisions based on sound commercial judgement. There could not have been a public sector operation better poised to move into the private sector, with a Board ready, willing and able to do so.

CHAPTER FIVE – IT WASN'T ALL PLANNING

The sense that the top management of the Company was getting to grips with the problems and changing the Company to respond to current market requirements had a remarkable effect on the line management. A type of leadership emerged that was prepared to make decisions and then stand by them in implementation. The Summerbreak holiday product was being sold very heavily and all previous records were broken. By the end of the year, it appeared that Winterbreak was going to do the same. This was achieved by a dramatic improvement in the quality of the brochure presentation, hard selling and careful preparation and timing of publicity material. On the selling front in America, we secured the Golf Tour Agency of British Airways and set up a well co-ordinated, efficient sales unit in New York. This, again, in 1979 beat all its previous selling records in North America.

First inroads were made into the destruction of the classic, tired hotel dining room. It was acknowledged that lunchtime business was changing and, whilst there was still a call for the sophisticated up-market lunch, in the main the volume business did not lie in that area and it was believed that it would never return. Self-service buffet luncheons were introduced and in several cases the special single dish lunch meal was developed.

Possibly the biggest change achieved was the introduction of the L'Entrecote Restaurant in the Great Eastern Hotel. The main architect of the thinking behind that development was Prudence Leith who worked tirelessly to guide and encourage staff to get the product to the standard we required. L'Entrecote was a simple theme. The meal began with a green salad, the main dish was steak with French fries and followed by an apple pie sweet. Wine was placed on the table with the selling style of asking if the customer wished it to be opened. There was a small range of wine available should a customer find that on the table was not to his liking but our objective was to have 100 covers capacity, selling at about £6.00 per head and certainly serve 100 covers a day. The response was incredible. There was no question of a slow build up of the volume; within two or three weeks it had arrived and the principal comment from the customers, completely missing the marketing objective, was to ask why we only charged £6.00 a head for a meal of that quality in those surroundings when we could easily charge £10.00 per head. Our answer really was quite simple that we would sooner have 100 customers at £6.00 a head than 40 at £10.00 a head.

In September 1979, we ran the European Open Golf Championship at Turnberry which was a most successful promotion exercise. Sadly, due to the strike of ITV at the time, the whole of the television coverage was lost; but a golf tournament of the European standard draws worldwide publicity and following only two years after the Open at Turnberry, it was a major contribution to confirm Turnberry and its golf courses as a location of international standing.

On the administrative front, the accountants had worked hard to produce a scheme for profit centre management and this was introduced by stages through the Company. It was a significant achievement in the line management of BTH where product management had played a much more significant role than business management and the response was most encouraging. Head waiters, chefs, receptionists all quickly understood the profit yardstick and sometimes were embarrassingly enthusiastic in achieving it.

About this time, London achieved the reputation of being the European rip off city and, to a certain extent, it was an honest label. But BTH was at the point of completing its development with the Grosvenor Victoria, where the objective was £10.00 per person per night accommodation in a shared room with private bath, colour television and Continental breakfast served in the room. The volume in the hotel was soon up to the expected level and the opening of the final floor to make it a 360 bedroomed hotel was awaited with enthusiasm. So much so that we began to study carefully where there may be other opportunities. It is a type of operation that is suitable where there is a high tourist throughput and, whilst one considered the possibility of further development in London, we looked to the provinces for short-term opportunity. The biggest second destination for tourists is Edinburgh and we had in Edinburgh a site at the back of the Caledonian Hotel where we believed it would be possible to get planning permission to enable a substantial development to take place though at that stage we were not certain whether development should be on the lines of the London Grosvenor Victoria or whether it should have one hotel at one end of Princes Street that was upper market and possibly the North British which sits on Waverley Station as the tourist type of hotel.

A small but very significant response was made to staff proposals when the grounds staff at Tregenna Castle in Cornwall put together a scheme to enable the 9-hole par three golf course at that hotel to be developed into an 18-hole course which they were prepared, given the necessary finance, to do themselves.

It was plain that we would never create a championship golf course at Tregenna Castle. Indeed, perhaps we didn't ever want to do since that hotel is eminently suitable for family holidays where perhaps one does not want serious golf to be played. The staff thought they were asking for the world in the figure of £10,000. This we readily found and it has been a great joy over the ensuing years to see a very pretty golf course develop at that hotel, for £10,000 and a lot of enterprise from the staff.

The booking system was delightfully antiquated and, whilst the Company did not wish to rush into computerising everything, particularly with the knowledge of errors made by competitors, we did decide that it was desirable to introduce a system in one or more of the major hotels, and a start was made for a computerised booking system at the Charing Cross to be followed by the Midland Manchester.

It was stimulating for the staff to see the Egon Ronay Lucas Guide reference to the Company's "exceptional standard of hotel keeping and impressive restaurants which we have praised for 24 years, are steeped in tradition and provide invaluable training background. Their staff, particularly their kitchen brigades enjoy rare esprit de corps. An exception amongst hotel chains they strike a happy balance between high quality and good profits without leaning unduly towards the latter. If British Transport Hotels were sold to a chain their standards would be brought down to a lower denominator."

On the Retail and Catering front, two new very high standard catering units were opened; one at King's Cross and the other at Paddington but the most important break through was to complete negotiations to take over the Wellington public house adjacent to Waterloo which, for the first time, enabled the Company to have a presence away from an actual railway station, though of course our legal advisers had to be satisfied that we could defend ourselves if attacked by those wishing to complain that we had exceeded our legal rights by trading off railway premises.

The Malmaison Wine Club achieved a turnover which, in real terms, more than doubled on the previous year and we appeared to have consolidated our position at the top of the wine business.

A major event of 1979 in the field of Train Catering was the centenary celebration which gave a new impetus to the business and was a fine morale booster. Public interest was shown and the media coverage gained a very favourable impression with the public. It was a pleasant change for the media not to be attacking but joining us in enjoying a hundred years of train catering history and admiring that achievement.

In addition, there were many, many examples of the Company really motivating itself; a house magazine was launched, staff sporting activity was developed, the Joint Consultative Council with the Trade Unions was inaugurated;

there was a conference at the NUR Headquarters with the NUR Executive and permanent Officers who were concerned with the BTH business.

As the head of the line management I became concerned at the amount that was being achieved and felt it was desirable to ensure that people really thought in a disciplined way about the organisation they were building up. It was decided to employ the consultants Harbridge House to work with the senior team to ensure that a thorough understanding of the philosophy behind the organisation changes was being achieved. This was a successful and very interesting way of making management think. We did not organise this on the basis of a single course but as a consultation of six days over a period of three months to ensure that management was constantly thinking about their tasks, not just having one spurt and then going home to bad habits. It was very important to have constructive thought out action.

At the end of 1979, we had achieved a great deal. We had planned a great deal and the future, given normal commercial disciplines, was extremely exciting.

CHAPTER SIX – FORMATION OF BRITISH RAIL INVESTMENTS LTD (BRIL)

The early months of 1980 produced much toing and froing as to how private sector money was to be made available for the Company and its fellow subsidiaries of British Rail. We needed to progress but it seemed that we had to first sit and wait. There began to be noticeable failure to appreciate that delay was a serious factor in the major task of running the business. All attention was on the Political issue and soon it became obvious that there were two distinct camps. Under the leadership of the BR Board there was a group seeking the best commercial development of the assets and, quite separately, there was a political/bureaucratic camp who were seeking to achieve a disposal objective in the most defendable light. This was probably a predictable position to the more Politically aware and merely reflected one group of people with commercial and business objectives as their goal and another group of people who were concerned with collecting 'brownie points' in their political and bureaucratic careers. It was well proven that the political/bureaucracy camp concealed any understanding they had of the business objectives that motivated those in command of the assets. Thus, of the two polarised positions, it became imperative in those early months of 1980 to ensure the decision taking process of private sector involvement was held by British Rail. Whilst the dangers of forming a holding company directed by the Secretary of State were well understood within the organisation, they were also very well set out in an excellent paper by the research staff of the National Union of Railwaymen and by others who had observed this standard solution over the years. There was an inevitability that BR would not be allowed to direct us in the introduction of private sector cash simply because of bias against Railways and its management, the reason for which was never clear.

Mr Norman Fowler, the Secretary of State for Transport, announced the formation of a holding company one hundred per cent owned by British Rail. The Minister saw the need to ensure that the enterprises would operate on equal terms with competitors in their respective markets which, it was argued, they were not able to do under public ownership. This was a repeat of an age old argument, the sincerity of which is rather weak. It is the system, the rules of which are set by the Government and the interference from politicians and bureaucrats that prevents the companies operating on equal terms with their competitors, it is not the method of ownership.

A determined Government could correct the position at the proverbial stroke by assuming the role of normal shareholders. Mr Fowler saw "the policy I have outlined will provide significant new opportunities for the subsidiary companies to develop and expand their businesses" and went on to confirm that British Rail "will certainly be able to maintain an investment in the subsidiaries". In response to a question during his statement, Mr Fowler repeated that the whole point "of what we are doing is to encourage the growth of businesses" and saw the advantage of the proposals to BR in that the proceeds for any disposals and the dividends from any investment would go to the account of British Rail.

Provided the Politicians could deliver what the Minister had said and ensure the bureaucracy worked to a similar end, there was nothing that need cause alarm to the staff, the Unions or the customers of the Company. The Board and senior management all wanted to see private sector investment and a freedom to operate on a commercial basis in free competition with the industry but many of us had been associated with the system and establishment over a number of years and were suspicious that meanings were being managed merely to overcome today's political pressures and that politicians would be 'on their bikes' when it suited them. We knew that BR and BTH Boards were fighting for similar ends but in BTH we knew that our parent was tied to the government. It was itself very unlikely to find any way to enjoy private sector freedom. How strong its Board would be against its political bosses was not clear. In the hotels and catering business there was no reason at all for political overtones to be applied to the management.

I called a meeting of the sixty most senior managers in the Company and explained how we would try to make what the Secretary of State had said come to fruition. At that meeting I explained, with full support, the Secretary of State's statement, explaining that neither the British Railways Board nor the Hotels had any option but to change and, what is more, we wanted to change in order to get investment into our business so that we could take advantage of development opportunities. We need no longer be tied to political decisions concerned with future policies for rail transportation in the country. Particularly, I emphasised the battle that BRB had fought and won over many months and, if nothing else, they had won a breathing space before subsequent fighting since the Holding Company would enable BR to retain control over the way in which private capital was introduced.

The Press were interesting in their comments. The Financial Times saw it "as a victory for commercial good sense over ideological rigidity" that struck "a sensible balance between the interest of tax payers, BR customers, employees and potential investors." It was the new holding company making disposals, initiating joint ventures, selling shareholdings in subsidiaries as and when commercial circumstances suggested this. It warned, "there will be a temptation for the government to use most of the proceeds of privatisation simply to reduce the public sector borrowing requirement by cutting BR's external financing cash limits by the amount of capital it raises through asset sales". Shrewd observations indeed, or was it premonition!

The Guardian saw it as "a considerable tactical victory for Sir Peter Parker the BR Chairman" and emphasised that Mr. Fowler had stressed that BR would "maintain substantial minority interests in all the companies through a wholly owned holding company". This however was against the banner headline, "BR Ferries and Hotels for Sale".

The Economist saw "embattled Board of BR" having won its fight with the Government to go about hiving off some of its non railway business in its own way. It believed that Treasury Ministers were pushing hard for BR to be forced immediately to set up a private sector holding company and that the Transport Minister had come down in BR's favour in allowing railwaymen to set up their own wholly owned umbrella group for non rail business.

In arguments with politicians, the bureaucracy or trade unions, I dislike seeing victors proclaimed. I am intensely motivated to achieve my objective but to have such achievement proclaimed as victory over the Establishment is dangerous. Rarely does the Establishment lose, because time is always on its side!

The Hotel Company Board was reasonably well contented with the conclusion that had been reached but was anxious now to test the ability of the politicians and bureaucrats to deliver and see how the Board of British Rail Investments Limited was to be constituted and whether they would make commercial judgement their criterion or just wilt under political pressure.

British Rail Investments Limited (BRIL) set to work to write its terms of reference and finally succeeded in getting a document to its subsidiaries in June 1981. The two prime objectives were defined in that document as being to enable the subsidiaries to expand and develop and to remove from the subsidiaries existing public sector controls on borrowing to finance investment, absence of which in the past had inhibited competitive performance and growth. They took unto themselves certain controlling responsibility which, whilst in principle was reasonable, in practice was just impossible because they had no staff. Whilst no-one wanted to see another tier of management emerge, it was of no advantage for the subsidiaries if BRIL were weak and ineffective in controlling or protecting them. Weakness in BRIL would soon enable the bureaucrats to use time to achieve the solution that was most easily defended politically which was to sell off the assets, thus neutering completely the achievement of the BR Board in controlling the Holding Company. It was essential to make bureaucrats implement the Secretary of State's statements in Parliament and that was going to need some high quality, determined staff work. The BRIL Board was chaired by Mr. J. M. W. Bosworth, the Vice Chairman of British Rail, a most highly respected individual admired not only for his skill but also for the incredible amount of work he was willing to undertake. There was one member of the Board of each subsidiary companies and then two nominees of the Secretary of State.

Looking back, it was a big mistake by BRIL not to staff themselves properly. It would have been unpopular at the time but the right compromise was not achieved in the staffing of the BRIL Headquarters. It started with its only permanent staff being a surplus person from the Pensions Department who was followed by a surplus person from the Property Company and finally by a surplus person from the Hovercraft Company. None of these people had the ability, the experience or the personality to do the task that had to be done. Their position was made totally impossible by the secondment to BRIL of enthusiastic young professionals from professional accountants and merchant bankers. BRIL had the task of making the Secretary of State's words stick against a bureaucracy with no past rules on which to base their decisions and they failed. It was penny pinching pound foolish at its worst.

The Company had the development plan that it had written in 1979 which, due to the distraction of the formation of BRIL and to a certain extent the consequent lack of interest of British Railways Board, just could not be made to materialise. The problems of not being allowed to invest actually became more acute and management had to use every trick in the book (and we knew plenty) to ensure that minor capital works were properly carried out. In the sense of planning, 1980 had become a complete wilderness. Authority to implement the new financial structure agreed by the BR Board was cancelled; no development of a corporate entity was allowed and the beginnings of a nervousness regarding the future of the Travellers-Fare part of the business emerged.

As had been stated earlier, the BTH Board were not exactly waiting to have their thinking stimulated on how to involve private sector finance. We had already had many discussions with different people and were therefore quite ready, soon after the announcement of BRIL, to put our first proposals to the test.

There were two proposals. The first was with another hotel company of slightly smaller size with a public quotation where we planned to sell to the quoted company a number of our hotels in exchange for shares and cash in that company to enable a substantial minority holding to be achieved. The quoted company would then lease to BTH the hotels that it had purchased plus all the properties presently operated by the quoted company. Thus, British Rail, through a minority holding in a quoted company, considerably expanded and created the development opportunity for its hotel company. BTH would become a company with few capital assets but a significant equity, easily disposable, could continue to be held in the quoted company. BTH would have emerged as the operators of practically 50 hotels, instead of 29 and would be able to demonstrate the implementation of the Secretary of State's plan for expansion and development. The idea was discussed with Trade Union leaders who readily agreed. The step need not have involved the whole company and could, therefore, have been the pilot for the first of several joint ventures that the company could undertake with other operators in the private sector.

The second proposal concerned Edinburgh. In addition to the land behind the Caledonian Hotel, owned by the Company and free for development, there was the North British Hotel at the other end of Princes Street which needed capital investment. We had under our belt the successful development of the Grosvenor Hotel in London as a high quality three-star tourist hotel. We took the view that the North British Hotel, sitting on the top of a railway station and adjoining a planned local authority development, was an ideal opportunity for a similar development in the second tourist city of Great Britain. In order to finance that proposal we had, in conjunction with the Bank of Scotland, carried out a market survey for the likely hotel need for Edinburgh and on the back of such report had obtained their support for financing the developments. The two hotels in Edinburgh could have been put into one separate company and that company thus divorced from public sector.

These two proposals were put to the Department of Transport officials in August 1980 and whilst it soon became painfully clear that they did not have the comprehension of these kind of entrepreneurial developments, more distressing was the revelation of a total lack of knowledge they had as to the rules that were to be set for privatisation. They could not move without Treasury instruction and it seemed that the Mandarins had not yet stirred! We were set to respond to a Political initiative and struck solid rock because the Department did not know the rules of the game they had been told to play.

The relationship between risk, ownership and control began to confuse officials as they interpreted government requirements to remove all three from BR and themselves. It was difficult to make them understand the difference between control and ownership and management. The fear began to be seen of a major shareholder with say, for example, 20% ownership when the remaining 80% is owned by say 10,000 shareholders. There was complete inability to understand the difference between management and control and that control probably reflected a financial risk whereas management need not.

If we were allowed to sell the property and take it back on a long lease, this probably would be included in the balance sheets of BTH and BR. It was then considered that government would therefore be guaranteeing the rent of the premises. I often wonder how many of my opposite numbers in the private sector were similarly diverted from the task of running their business.

Further confusion was created by the officials endeavouring to draw a line one side of which was described as significant expansion and development and the other side of which was described as insignificant. The purpose of this was never clear because the Secretary of State had not indicated that he wished to place any constraints on the amount of expansion or development and certainly had not done so in his statements to the House of Commons. However, they were the people with his ear and with the power to influence him and the first of our ideas was considered to be acceptable so far as the amount of expansion was concerned but defeated on the grounds that control would not be seen to pass. The second was defeated on the grounds that it was too large an expansion project. There were many, many meetings with civil servants at various levels as we tried to assemble some sort of rules within which we could have elbow room to actually do something. The longer the discussions went on, the more clear it became that there was precious little business urgency being brought to bear on the implementation of the political initiative. They found it necessary, but impossible, to define the point at which risk was removed from the public sector, yet wanted to hold up any development on the grounds that risk has not passed. There was total confusion between ownership, control and management and the Civil Servants were unable to give any guidelines that we could use to plan our future.

The most distressing factor was the fact that managing a business of 10,000 people caused not the slightest concern to Politicians, Treasury or Department officials as they were protecting the flanks of their particular interests. We were managing a large business while they were doing a case study!

CHAPTER SEVEN – THE PROSPECTUS
DISTRACTION

Towards the end of August 1980, the BR Board cash position was reaching a crisis point. They had to act desperately and, even before BRIL had taken its first breath, one of the solutions that was being considered as a help to the cash limit problem of BR was to sell the total BT Hotels activity.

This position was reported to the BTH Board Meeting on 10th September 1980 and, not unnaturally, the non-executive members of the Board expressed their deep concern that the Board was not being consulted and that discussions between the BRB and the Department of Transport would not, therefore, be reflecting the views of the members of the Board. Whilst the directors of the Company had always endorsed the proposal for the setting up of a Holding Company wholly owned by BRB, they considered it vital that the Company be granted such freedoms as are necessary to enable it to compete on equal terms with the privately owned sector of the hotel industry. In particular, the Company required the right to retain funds obtained as the result of the sale of assets so that investment could be made in the remaining and new assets. The BTH Board wanted to behave in a businesslike manner and, if that meant winding up the company, they would not hesitate to do so but, to be told of a possible sale to enable financial targets of a loss making part of the total was rather off-hand to put it mildly, particularly since the increasing cash flow problems in BR were due to Industrial Relations problems in respect of railway operations. It was like mortgaging the house to pay the food bills and having no idea what you were going to sell for the next food bill. Possibly, in hindsight, the early stages of the national policy of subsequent years and referred to in a speech in the Lords by an elder and respected Politician.

The Press, the previous week, had carried a report that British Railways Board had, as a result of its current financial difficulties, engaged Morgan Grenfell to prepare a prospectus document for the sale of the total BTH activity. The directors of BTH expressed the view that to sell 29 hotels against a specified deadline could only be made at what was described as a distress discount. The directors expressed their desire to see the Chairman of British Railways Board as a matter of urgency in order to express their views.

This meeting took place on 16th September and it was during that meeting that the Chairman was called to the telephone to receive a message from the Permanent Secretary that there would be increase of the order of £40m. to the cash limits set for BT for 1980/81.

This is typical of the way the Chairman of British Rail was having to live. He had the Board of one of his subsidiaries trying to act in a business way, responding to the businesslike leadership he was wishing to impose on the whole of BR, yet was having to control radical changes in the whole of his command to meet the requirements of the April year end of the Treasury Cash Book. Long term business evolution does not actually have regard to the Treasury mandarins or indeed their fiscal year. Successful change is a long term, carefully controlled evolution in which the phase of the moon has little significance.

The outcome of the meeting was that any work on a prospectus should be stopped and not even reconsidered for three months and that BTH should, in the light of its own capital investment requirements, dispose of the wine business and the laundry business, complete its Edinburgh project and examine the possibility of Gleneagles by itself becoming a private sector company. All of these matters were in hand but progress was interrupted by this diversion and the time it took to convince our merchant bank advisers that we had some control over our destiny and we were being supported by our Parent.

On 30th September 1980, the first meeting was held with officials of the Bank of Scotland and British Linen Bank in respect of the last two items and it is from that meeting that Gleneagles Hotels plc was born. Meanwhile, some work that had been started early in August 1980 had come to fruition. The Board of BTH had invited Morgan Grenfell to undertake the task of advising on value of the Gleneagles Hotel, assuming that its business were to be owned as a separate company with the majority of the shares being held by the public at large. The Board found it difficult to accept their opinion that, if a flotation of Gleneagles alone were considered with BR owning a significant minority then, such a company would be valued at only £2.4m.

Morgan Grenfell were the financial advisers to the Board and clearly their advice could not be dismissed lightly but, on this occasion, the BTH Board did not agree with it and in their view decided that no further action would be taken upon the idea of trying to put Gleneagles to the market as a single entity. The problem in Scotland was beginning to be more clear cut in that there were three hotels, all very large, within close proximity of each other and in the main tourist centre of Scotland. The North British Hotel, Edinburgh, was in desperate need of refurbishment and, in our view, conversion to a three-star good quality tourist type hotel; the Caledonian which was in need of a face-lift with substantial area to its rear which was capable of being developed in conjunction with the local authority; and Gleneagles where there was a good profit base on which to build but where an investment of the order of £400,000 to £500,000 was desirable to complete the work we had started.

The wine business in which the Company had such high national repute was a greater consumer of cash. Very large stocks had to be held and the company had to consider carefully whether or not it was in business to promote and provide an excellence in wine or whether its business was to sell wine. There was no doubt in the minds of the Board that the objective was to sell wine. So, whilst it was desirable to implement the decision to dispose of the business, it was more important to work hard at a programme of reducing the stocks which, at this time were well over £3m.

There were three laundries in the Company, all no doubt a very good idea at the time when they had been built. The amount of investment needed in order to preserve their efficiency was high and had it been carried out the capacity would have been greatly in excess of domestic requirements. The legal problems of working for third parties were no nearer a solution.

The year of 1980 ended in a blaze of meetings, trying to explain how we were trying to implement the Government policy to the Secretary of State and his Minister on 3rd November; to the leaders of the NUR on 25th November and later the same day to the leaders of the Transport Salaried Staff Association; on 27th November to the NUR and TSSA sponsored members of Parliament; on 1st December to the Travel Writers Press and, finally, on 10th December to the Board of BRIL as it made its fact-finding tour of the subsidiary companies.

It may seem surprising, but it is nevertheless true that BRIL members who were available made their fact-finding tour on 10th December. Of itself, not an unreasonable time scale related to the date the Secretary of State announced its birth and the time it takes to formalise appointments. The incredible situation was that between those dates someone briefed Morgan Grenfell to prepare a prospectus and BR were given £40m additional cash that avoided the need for such work. The new BRIL Board members must have found it a strange business world into which they were moving with their assets being ordered for sale before they had actually had time to see them.

At the end of a traumatic year, there was no lack of enthusiasm from the BTH Board to succeed with the private sector finance but they were positioned somewhere between bemused and annoyed by the way so many people seemed to have, or believed they had, the rights to make decisions about the future and expect them quietly to nod their approval.

CHAPTER EIGHT – ACHIEVEMENTS OF 1980

Natural optimism makes everyone hope that the year just ended would prove to be the worst ever and this was certainly my hope at the end of 1980 which had been an exceptionally poor year for business. Whilst 1980 had been a bad year for the industry generally, we produced one of the worst profit performances of the Company's history. It was one in which we had achieved the greatest organisational change ever undertaken but our bottom line performance did not create strength. There is no doubt that implementation of the change had helped us weather the storms. It had been an exceptionally good distraction for the line management who would otherwise have been exceedingly depressed by the political influences that were being forced into the business and the constant media reporting that the Company was up for sale.

A new management style giving hitherto unknown authority and responsibility was in the Company. Some found it less enjoyable when no longer were "they" available to blame. Some senior changes had to be made as people had taken their opportunity to fail to respond to the new challenges.

Golf played a major part in the 1980 business and we successfully staged the Bob Hope Show/Amateur at Turnberry in September. We had two other significant first events; the PGA Seniors at Gleneagles in August and the PGA Club Professional Championship at Turnberry. We fought very hard to get these important golf promotions and the results were satisfactory. The new Glendevon Course was opened at Gleneagles and in August the new course at the Welcombe Hotel, Stratford, was opened with every indication that both of these courses would be commercially viable.

We had continued to encourage our chefs to participate in their professional competitions and, for the first time, we entered a team led by Chef Rogerson from Inverness to the Frankfurt International Exhibition and Competition. It was a great achievement to come home with six medals and further acknowledgement of Chef Rogerson's work when the Inverness Hotel dining room was awarded the AA rosette together with the Menu of the Year Award. Hotelympia produced seven gold medals, four silver and five bronze, a result for a single organisation probably only bettered by the Armed Services.

Our major hotel success was undoubtedly the Grosvenor Hotel, Victoria, which, having opened in one of the most difficult years of the past decade, achieved a room occupancy of 84%. In our attempt to promote the efforts of our Travellers-Fare activity and to get over the message that the curly sandwich was very dead, we were very proud of our achievement in opening the Casey Jones new fast food unit at Waterloo. By the end of the year, the turnover was exceeding £15,000 a week and we were encouraged in the thought that this could be the forerunner of a chain of such operations particularly, of course, if we could only remove the legal obstacle that prevented us from conducting our business in the high street. Here was a development that matched any competition but the law prevented us from exploiting it. A great credit must go in this successful development to the understanding between management and unions in dealing with a personnel problem that had never been tackled before in establishing the working arrangements in the Casey Jones unit.

We had, of course, the previous year successfully sneaked out on the high street with the Wellington Pub at Waterloo and it was pleasing to see the trade there trebled following the complete refurbishment we carried out when we took it over.

Three new restaurants were opened in the hotels with a garden room theme where we projected our objective of value for money with a service between 11.00a.m. and 10.30p.m. without closing. In Newcastle and in Hartlepool the fine spacious dining rooms exploited their Victorian sense of grandeur by the discreet introduction of a bar into the restaurant area.

The Turnberry Hotel Conference Centre was opened which, for its size, was as advanced as any in the country and, with the development of the small sports and leisure complex, Turnberry development was completed.

A very important step forward was achieved in the Train Catering Division where a contractual arrangement was set up between the division and the Chief Passenger Manager of British Rail for the operation of train catering services. This put the responsibility for the style of service into the Passenger Business and the Company had the great satisfaction of seeing that Division operate on a strictly profit orientated basis effectively as contractors to BR for the service. This was a totally new innovation by the Company and was a great credit to the management who implemented it so successfully. It placed the product objective responsibility where it belonged – in Railway Passenger management – and the Product performance responsibility in the Company.

The Malmaison Wine Club continued to flourish and its reputation was enhanced considerably by being voted the best buy by both Consumers' Association and Sunday Times.

Education, training and management development played a very important part in the work in 1980. At hotel management level the introduction of profit centres was a catalyst around which much of the management training was conducted.

A new innovation for in-house training was developed in which twelve people who were considered to have potential had been brought together for about six weeks spread over a period of eighteen months. Under the overall leadership of a very senior member of the Company, they worked and thought their way through a business project that was as broadly based as possible to force them into considering the matters that influence business outside of their immediate personal performance and the constraints of the Public Sector.

In New York, BTH Hotels Inc. was changed to be an independent business centre with a broader base for developing representation of other hotels and as a tour operator. During the year, it was moved from some rather undesirable offices in Queens' to a more satisfactory location in Manhattan, from which it began to make very significant sales contributions to the Company as it responded to the sharper management control exercised firmly by the Executive Directors of the Divisions.

Over several years we had endeavoured at stations to tap the vast retail market that exists around them and a survey in 1980 indicated that at our London grocery and off-licence shops half the customers were non-travellers. If only we could achieve the freedom to move outside the Railway stations, our now proven ability to run successful businesses in retail and catering could be developed.

Financially, 1980 was a disastrous year but we were not alone. The management of the Company responded to the challenge it could so clearly see and was pulling itself up by its proverbial bootlaces to ensure that when better times came along, it was ready to seize them.

CHAPTER NINE – THE WILDERNESS OF 1981

Whilst the BTH Board were anxious to break away from the public sector, they were an experienced body of people in the main being influenced by their backgrounds in the private sector. They saw the dangers of making progress on any basis other than that of sound commercial judgement. Political ideology or advancement was not part of the equation. British Rail Investments Limited was a compromise and at risk directly and indirectly of strong political direction. The politicians and bureaucrats had to prevent British Rail "getting away with it" by creating an organisation structure over which the Establishment had no influence. "It" with which BR might be seen to be trying to get away would probably make good commercial sense because the BR Board was strongly influenced by very experienced business people. Inevitably, therefore, we watched carefully as BRIL, now inserted between ourselves and BR, began to feel the need to get involved. BTH had been involved in discussions for over a year with different organisations and they now found themselves responding to an entirely new organisation who were having to concern themselves with writing their own terms of reference and trying to decide how they were going to be able to flex their muscles as the new bosses. The initiatives we had taken we were told must now be considered in relation to the policy which BRIL would be formulating and it was made abundantly clear that it was not considered appropriate for the BTH Board to take any initiative beyond the exploratory stage. We were asked to provide a framework of the current views and plans. It is disaster for any commercial or military operation to be told to stop while those responsible decide what to do.

Following the meeting in September 1980 between the Chairman of BR and several members of the BTH Board, the course of action that has been described was implemented. We had not subsequently been slovenly in meeting our commitments and, as a result, early in 1981 we were in a very advanced stage of the formulation of Gleneagles Hotels plc, Midland Hotels Limited, the sale of The Old Course Hotel in St. Andrews and the disposal of the Wines and Laundry Businesses. The enthusiastic youngsters who were seconded from leading professional firms seemed to be under the misapprehension that we had been waiting for their arrival and when they discovered this was not the case, believed everything should immediately stop until the BTH Board had received their recommendations. It really was the most incredible six months of diverting management attention away from the fairly major task of running the Company at a time when the markets were at the lowest ebb for twenty years.

The BTH Board warned BRIL of the danger of constant diversion of line management attention. It was well within the compass of a management team to run the business and at an appropriate pace make changes to introduce private sector finance. It was totally unreasonable to expect the management, in addition to teach the inexperienced set of people from BRIL about the business, correct their wrong impressions and then spend time arguing with their ideas how we should go about dealing with the privatisation issue. Management was in the position of dealing with people who had a great stock of classic solutions and who were seeking the problems to which they could apply them, with a desire to change the facts to be suitable to receive their "ex-stock" solution.

By April 1981, BRIL saw the magnitude of its problems and resorted to asking BTH to provide a framework of current views and plans. This was done and we explained that for more than a year, the Company had been thinking about ways and means of developing and expanding BTH in association with private sector finance. We acknowledged that BRIL must influence and direct that thinking and pointed out that it would be taking over something that had already begun, hoping that BRIL would find that what had been started was a sensible road to follow. The Company set down the fundamentals on which it had based its approach:-

(a)   the disposal of units that were considered to be beyond recovery;

(b)   to use its better assets as a base on which to raise funds for expansion;

(c)   to base proposals on sound business sense, emphasising that they are not proposals made to respond to any political directive;

(d)   that financially, the Company must be self-sufficient and make an appropriate return on all investment;

(e)   that provided it can meet good business criteria, the Company would continue as a business entity.

We then listed the main discussions that had taken place, to give some idea of the way the Board were endeavouring to change BTH to meet the requirements of a company of real standing in the hotel industry.

The thinking on Gleneagles Hotel plc, of which more is written later, was explained. The Board's preferred method of developing its Edinburgh property and consequently the best profit route for the Company was to borrow on the security of an asset. The Department would not allow that form of privatisation and, therefore, the second best route was chosen and the new company was in the final stages of being constructed.

For years, two hotels in Derby and Sheffield had been very poor performers and not the least reason was the lack of courage to invest in changing the product of those units. The market requirement of the localities had changed considerably and the style of hotel that BTH was trying to run in those cities was not the requirement of the market. An association was being formed with another hotelier in Derby who had already demonstrated good professional ability at the rather lower end of the market. A new company was being formed that would own the Midland Hotel, Derby and the Royal Victoria Hotel, Sheffield (both BT Hotels) and the Clarendon Hotel, Derby with a management that had the experience to change these hotels to respond to the market requirements.

The Adelphi in Liverpool had not made money for years. The amount of money needed for repairs could be justified. Competition had been allowed to develop in the City with Government grants. Liverpool had, and still has, enormous unemployment problems and, apart from the week of the Grand National, there was little to be made. Accordingly, the BTH Board had decided that this property was to go on the market but a quiet word had been spread that with the current situation in Liverpool, that British Railways Board would not be very popular if they were to dispose of that property and were commended to wait for a more suitable opportunity.

The Old Course Hotel at St. Albans had never been a success and, whilst many attempts had been made by changing its style and introducing winter closing, it could not be made into a profitable unit without substantial capital expenditure. The Old Course was a wonderfully sited hotel but needed to be something more than an up-market rooming house. The Board's thinking at that time was to develop the whole into time-sharing type of country club, many of which had flourished over the past decade. The home of golf was such an obvious location for a real up-market development on these lines.

We had spent a great deal of time endeavouring to join forces with another organisation in the wine trade to develop that business. The Company in its own name and through the Malmaison Wine Club has a very high reputation but its successful development demanded very high capital investment in liquid stock. There was an abundance of people on the look out for some cheap wine but not too many who were willing to join forces to make a real business venture or to buy our stock at a reasonable price.

The Laundries problem was classic in that very many years ago, railways developed facilities for dealing with dirty linen. Slowly they had failed to keep the resources up to date with modern development and the result was that the Company was faced with a severe investment problem, probably in the order of £3 million in one of its three locations. It was clear that at the other two locations within five years similar investment would be required. Whilst at the time of the initial investment this was no doubt a very sensible thing to have done, commercial laundries had developed over the years to such an extent that they could, with their specialisation, undertake the operation at a cheaper rate than we could possibly do it ourselves. There was, at that time, a firm proposal before the Board for the merging of our business with a publicly quoted company.

In addition to these firm positions, there were others well advanced in the exploratory stage. A property company was willing to purchase the properties and give the Company management contracts for their operation. There was discussion with another publicly quoted hotel company whose resources were very compatible with those of BTH where the merging of the two companies would have produced a formidable business. A very interesting discussion was going on with an American company who had three hotels in mainland Europe but nothing in the UK and were anxious to pursue an investment. Some of our properties were seen as being an attractive addition to a golf based hotel country club business.

Our report concluded making two major points. One was that the Company management was under extreme pressure in trying to do its job in running the business and that to meet its objective of reducing its labour force of 10,000 by one thousand was no mean task. The second major point it made was a plea that the Board should not be prevented from doing many smaller things that needed to be done and sought the authority to have delegated to it the power to take to finality any deal with the private sector provided this did not exceed £1/2 million.

The report was, no doubt, considered by the BRIL Board but certainly no strategy or policy materialised from that Board and, whilst such a comment can quite fairly be made, at the same time, it is only reasonable to consider the kind of problem that they were trying to handle. It became abundantly clear as time went on that they were merely the tomato in a sandwich with one layer of bread being subsidiary companies pressing them to give orders or to support a course that the management was proposing and the other slice of bread the dead hand of the politicians and bureaucrats, with a breadth of commercial vision limited to imposing a Political ideology timed totally to - "the lifetime of this Government" - completely incompatible with commercial judgement.

The Company had been formulating and constructing its plans for the Gleneagles Hotel Company since October 1980, working to an objective of consideration by the BTH Board at the end of March 1981. Six months is not an unreasonably long time in which to undertake a job of that magnitude even if there are no little hand grenades being thrown at you by those who you think might be on your side. After all, it was privatisation we were accomplishing, albeit on our own initiative. Our colleagues in BR and BRIL had been pursuing officials to endeavour to get some sort of clarity on the rules within which we could work but it wasn't until 15th January, that is practically two-thirds of the way through the time programme, that the Department put down what they saw as the way to "escape from the public sector" in a document they "hoped we would find helpful".

Clarity and help can be judged to some extent by the following extracts.

"The two basic criteria for deciding whether an economic unit is in or out of the public sector are control and ownership in that order. This is accepted internationally in the context of national accounting although the reverse order may seem more natural."

It seems reasonable to interpret that statement to be that control and ownership are separate, otherwise there is little point in arguing about the order, but a little later the explanation is:

"in broadest terms the corporate body is regarded as in the public sector if it is both controlled and owned by Government on a basis that is intended to be permanent".

Without being pedantic, it may be presumed that an economic unit and a corporate body are one and the same thing.

Ownership is, as they say in politics, "perfectly clear" but the word control begs a number of questions. We were helped to understand the meaning as "the kind of control which stems from general regulatory powers" and to be "over broad aspects of policy not day to day management seen as an active form of control and not merely as a passive reserve power to be used only in time of crisis." Two areas of the policy referred to are identified as "matters concerning capital investment and borrowing." Pricing policy was seen as a third area, especially if the Government generally were to accept responsibility for the financial consequences of intervening. In fairly simple terms, this meant that we were being told that regardless of our level of ownership in the Gleneagles Company, we must not exercise any control over the investment programmes of the Company, its financing arrangements or its pricing policy. It seems an extremely strange view to take on an investment to say that, when the nation is a shareholder, it should act in such a passive way regarding the affairs of the company in which it has invested. We were going to be required to fall over backwards to demonstrate that we had no control over the company's affairs, the appointment of its Board or its management.

The guide to how to escape from the public sector goes on to state the obvious that the simplest case to imagine is total disposal where the Government have no continuing liability to buyers and place no restrictions on their actions. But if there is not to be total disposal, the size of shareholding retained may be seen as significant in relation to intentions about control,

"generally speaking the smaller the residual shareholding of the Government, the easier to classify to the private sector. In any event satisfactory assurances about the withdrawal of control are necessary."

That is a most significant statement requiring us in any form of privatisation we undertook to give assurance that BTH withdrew from control. It really was the most devastating piece of news that could have been given to a Company and a Board, who had fought so hard to succeed in dragging itself up by its proverbial bootlaces to be told that whatever else it did it was not going to be allowed to exercise any managerial control. That really was the kiss of death. The Civil Servants were completely lost and unable to demonstrate the original thinking with a prize statement in the document

"the lack of precedent for privatisation make it hard to draw up precise rules".

Before going on to elaborate on the principles, we were told of

"a major problem you face is that of avoiding the symbiotic relationship between the Board and the privatised body."

That indeed caused many of us to rush for our Oxford Dictionaries. The elaboration was emphasising that there would be a requirement placed on the Board to demonstrate that there was no control being effected and the statement that the Department would want the Board to undertake that it would not use its dominant position to control the policy of the Company.

Had the matter not been so serious, it could have been amusing to read their conclusion that it was not suggested that the Board would find any particular difficulty in agreeing with the Department schemes which would introduce private capital into the subsidiaries in order to allow them to be classified as private sector. But the Department had felt it desirable to draw our attention to some of the constraints which exist so that in considering the proposals for introducing private capital into parts of the Board's business,

"we will be able to distinguish between schemes which are likely to run into trouble through the concept of symbiosis and those which are likely to be more fruitful."

There cannot be an entrepreneurial and dynamic Board in the whole of British industry that is not aware of the importance of avoiding symbiosis in the strategic development of its business! I hope my lengthy explanation goes some way to justifying my sympathy for the problem that BRIL were trying to face. Having started the Gleneagles project the previous October, we had reached the point of being somewhat concerned about the complete lack of guidance on the political requirements being given by the bureaucrats. They had no experience upon which to form judgements themselves as to a sensible route except of course, the simple one of sell the lot. Perhaps the position would not have been so bad had the BTH Board not been extensively experienced in the private sector. There was a wealth of knowledge of the options that were available, there was ability to select a good commercial option but there was no power to implement.

Throughout all of these discussions, the BTH management had been working in close co-operation with British Linen Bank and other professionals advisers. The scheme that was now in the final stages of drafting was considered by the team to be a good commercial proposal which would have backing from the City. In addition, we had a great Political ploy which was to involve the Secretary of State for Scotland to ensure that the proposals had his support. This was done by creating the philosophy of this being a new Scottish company and everything concerned with its launch was done in Scotland. This achieved its objective but, like all ploys of that nature, had repercussions because eventually people believed us and we found ourselves swept along on the wave that there must be a Scotsman to be Chairman and only Scotsmen could really know how to run that company. The point of the work of the team was to establish a commercially viable company that would be financially well supported and have a strong management team. Foolishly, perhaps, we thought that this would also be the objective of the bureaucrats but, alas, they were more concerned with interpreting the Treasury guidelines and considering whether the project fell within the concessions described in the Monk report to the Nationalised Industries Chairmen's Group in February of 1980, and we began a round of arguments as to whether the fact that over 50% of equity and more than the prescribed 40% of the balance sheet were in the ownership of the private sector. Having satisfied themselves on those two counts, doubts were expressed as to whether the draft proposals would permit the Treasury to let the Company exist outside of the external financing limits of BR because the rates of interest on the proposed unsecured loan stock could possibly be considered low and thus interpreted as a gross subsidisation from BTH to Gleneagles plc and also, because the scheme as we had put it together, enabled BTH, by the system of share warrants to increase its shareholding if the enterprise was successful. This was seen to run counter to expectations inherent in the whole concept that future finance should be raised on the market. That is to say that if the Government invested in a company and that company was successful, political dogma was demanding that any future increase in the capital of that company should normally be raised on the market and not from existing shareholders as right. (A very interesting viewpoint that subsequently reared its head in the middle of 1983 with significant effect on the ownership of the company.)

Additionally, it was questioned whether the company could be classified as private sector unless there was clear specification regarding the number of directors and the spread of shareholders. Slowly, it became clear that, in spite of having carried the major load with two of our non executive directors of putting together this private sector deal, the line management of BTH was going to have no say whatsoever in the running of the company of which it was going to be the major shareholder.

On our behalf and in common business sense, the Deputy Chairman of BR, who was Chairman of BTH and now Chairman of BRIL, Mr. J M W Bosworth, was carrying the brunt of these discussions with the bureaucrats. What a predicament the man was in since his BTH team, with their professional advisers, had now completed the work, meetings had taken place with potential investors and it was believed that there was sufficient backing for the scheme to be placed in the market. On 20th March the Department wrote to acknowledge the many discussions that had taken place between myself and Arthur Brooking on the one side and Patrick Brown and Jennie Page on the other and understood that we were now going to rework the proposals so that a new version of the scheme could be sent "within the next few days". They said that they would "do all we can to see that the necessary further discussions within Government take place as quickly as possible." They did not understand that we were actually trying to implement something and that those being encouraged to provide finance were not terribly concerned with the finer points of Political ideology and the management of the meanings of the Treasury mandarins. Investors were concerned with putting their money into a good commercial project and they saw one in front of them. The crushing bureaucrat comment was that they thought it fair to warn us that they could not guarantee speedy approval for any scheme on the lines that they had already seen and even if it was modified in the way they had suggested, the scheme would be unlikely to be classified as private sector and thus outside of the Board's external financing limits. "A more clear cut disposal of ownership and control would not run into the difficulties which I see may face the GHL proposals". The letter concluded by reminding us that we would undoubtedly need to take account in continuing discussions with merchant banks and potential investors of the likely need for some time for consideration once the scheme was submitted for Ministerial approval.

This was really the straw that would break any camel's back. After six months' dedicated work with first class professional advisers, we had a scheme which we were convinced would succeed if it were put to investors and we found ourselves confronted with a philosophy that was simply saying ask the investors to wait while we work out our departmental problems. This led to the Chairman of BRIL, with the full support of the Chairman of BR, breaking every rule in the book and going straight to the Secretary of State, pointing out that we had by now spent £300,000 putting a privatisation scheme together; we had spent many months of management time and now the rules were being changed in the middle of play and, unless there were urgent discussions, the whole project would be in jeopardy. It is quite impossible to create innovative schemes when the Treasury persists in trying to find a common solution, rules within which they always win and totally ignoring the way that deals of this nature to be put together with great flexibility and usually on a short lead time in the decision taking stages.

As has been said several times, and certainly acknowledged by Sir Peter Parker, there was the important problem that the management had to consider to deal with the day to day running of the company as an integral part of the Corporate Plan for BR. This, of course, is handled by exactly the same members of the Department who were at that time having a fairly testing time with the Treasury on the matters that have been described. The thinking of the BTH Board was that it would be continuing to run a very substantial hotel business, taking full advantage of the opportunity to use private sector money and, after all that is what the Secretary of State had said. It was quite clear about the various options that were commercially sensible for it to follow.

Against this background it did not seem unreasonable to the BTH Board to presume that it would be continuing to invest at least at the same level of funding that was being provided by its depreciation provisions. It had no silly ideas that it would go seeking Government money to buy a whole new range of hotels but this point could never be understood by the Department who, on 9th April, expressed their concern that the Board should permit a planning assumption that there would be no constraints on investment. They saw this as unrealistic and believed that "any planned new investment should be met by the private sector at the time that it was required and if it were not then it was to continue to be part of the financing limits of BR". The key point of such an argument is that none of the money that we were able to raise as a result of the kind of package we had put together for the Gleneagles Company could be redeployed by the BTH Board. All money raised must be considered as part of the external financing limits of BR. But the Secretary of State, replying to questions on 3rd June, (Hansard 912/13) said that he hoped BR would use its realised funds to invest in more hotels.

So concerned were the Department's Officers about any BTH plan that presumed investment that they required an assessment to be made of the impact on the performance of the business of the continuance of existing constraints on finance and investment so that the Government could have a view of the results of continuing restriction and so "produce a genuine baseline against which other alternatives can be evaluated". The planning letter from the Ministry concluded that the writer did not think "there were any other issues of importance on the BTH Plan raised in our discussion but if you disagree no doubt you will let me know". The reality of the situation is well put in a Minute from the BR Board Member for Finance to his Director of Planning "in practice this issue may not arise since experience with recent BTH Plans has shown that the key determinant of 'what the business can afford' has contained investment level". It was encouraging to find that there were still people about who understood the basic concepts of running a business.

CHAPTER TEN - RAILWAYS ACT TO PROTECT TRAVELLERS-FARE

It is worth recalling that early in 1978 the Railways Board had decided that there would be a single business developed out of the hotel and catering activities. There was never any doubt in the minds of those of us who were concerned with running the business that this was the right course. Whilst we all reacted with the enthusiasm of a management receiving clear directives from its parent, only the cynics spoke of the danger of that management support being withdrawn because of expediency in responding to political change. We were still of the belief that the British Railways Board was in control of its destiny. We had faith in those in control and were prepared to react in support of that more senior management group.

The first test of strength and determination to achieve its declared objective was placed on the Railways Board early in 1979 when the proposed organisation structure to enable the whole business to develop on the lines they required was submitted for their approval. There was slightly less enthusiasm than my line management would have liked for the bringing together of the two businesses for which BTH was responsible. The Travellers Fare Board was clearly seen as a power base the appointment to which, and certainly the Chairmanship of which, was not to be relinquished easily. The Board required Messrs.

Bosworth and Reid to submit their organisation proposals early in 1980 by which time two years had elapsed since the BR Board had indicated the direction in which it wished the hotels and catering businesses to move. That was weakness and since it effectively was inviting Bob Reid to propose his own removal as Chairman of Travellers Fare, was unlikely to result in achieving the Board's 1978 objective.

The new organisation structure was beginning to bite and on the Travellers-Fare side we had, in Jack Simpson and David Bailey, two men who had satisfactorily proved their ability to take command as the Executive Director of the Train Catering Division and Retail and Catering Division respectively. Such a move would then leave us free to appoint Bill Currie the Operations Director of the whole Company, a job for which he was both well trained and experienced.

In March 1980, I put forward my proposals for the organisation of Travellers-Fare against the background of already having achieved a contractual relationship between the Train Catering Division and the railway operational management in respect of catering on trains and having established a normal landlord and tenant arrangement in respect of establishments of the Retail and Catering Division.

We had, over a short period of time, established a semi arm's length relationship with our colleagues in the railway and established Travellers-Fare as an integral part of a single company concerned with hotels and catering. With these under our belt, it was logical to propose the disbandment of the Travellers-Fare Board that had been set up some years earlier. In order to ensure that there would be proper liaison with BR, it was proposed that the Retail and Catering Divisional Executive should be strengthened by representatives of the BR Property Board and the Passenger Sales Manager and that the Train Catering Divisional Executive should be strengthened by the addition of the Inter City Passenger Manager. These two developments were designed to help railway operators in their decisions over what was to be provided and in support of their services. Whilst it was very much welcomed in informal discussion by those down the line responsible for the operations, it was immediately seen as a loss of power by the people who had been concerned with such committees as the Travellers-Fare Divisional Board. There was never any proposition that senior Railway Board Members should be removed from the BTH Board.

The success of Messrs. Simpson and Bailey, their personal strengths and the contract and tenancy arrangements, all created a fear that control was within an ace of being lost to railway operators. Relationships were different but were no less loyal.

In classic style, the best delaying tactics were employed and two further reports were commissioned. The first was known as the Ellison Report and was published at the end of April 1980. This was not at all helpful to those who wished to procrastinate or find support for an argument against direction in which the BRB wished to develop in early 1978. Ellison had two problems: he was a man who understood the problem and was inclined to speak his mind. The conclusions were not very different from our own and so there was very little argument. This Report, following one meeting in May 1980, died its natural death and a further report was commissioned which became known as the Lewin Report. This was published in November 1980 and missed more points than it made. It was received so badly by people at the Centre that it did not even form the basis for any subsequent discussion. In some respects that was slightly unreasonable since a lot of work had gone into the paper and whilst many of its arguments were not based on good fact, the effort was worthy of some discussion. Procrastination won, for by the end of 1980 the parent, BRB, had little comfort in its policy declaration of three years earlier because new Political pressure for privatisation and a state of deep concern was developing in many people's minds as to how the Railway could insulate itself from any private sector developments. The BTH Board must have been seen in some respects as a godsend and in others as a great danger.

A godsend in the sense that they were seeing all the opportunities that could arise by getting themselves free from the bureaucracy but, on the other hand, a danger because such enthusiasm expressed as part of BR could risk private sector involvement in railway station operations and also in the operations on the trains themselves. The waverers could see the only solution to that problem as some form of segregation of Travellers-Fare from the remainder of BTH. That is to say, a complete reversal of the policy that the Board had decided to be right early in 1978. Political influence became dominant over business judgement.

It is interesting to recall, also about this time, a matter which put BTH Board at loggerheads with the Centre as it pursued objectives to having a successful business. At the time I came into the Company, there was a programme for the introduction of computerised control into Travellers-Fare by the BR Computer Services Department. The ideas were complex but undoubtedly very sound. I discovered on arrival that of the implementation time of three years, two had elapsed. We were approximately one year behind schedule and getting worse. I began to insist on firm targets for those responsible for the computer programmes and after a further year, as delays got worse and worse, enough was enough, and decisions had to be taken to cut losses and take another course to achieve the same objectives. Those in charge of this technical development within Travellers-Fare, together with its senior executives, made recommendations to me for an alternative course.

They made proposals which were not only cheaper but ones which could be implemented by a professional firm within six months. Such recommendation caused a rumpus and a half in BR. After several discussions and finally a table-thumping meeting with Bob Reid, he decided that we were to continue on the BR path. Once again, the path for independence had been hampered. It was sad to hear in due course, a very senior finance man say that two years and £1 million later they were starting to implement what had been proposed. I do not make the point in any way to prove that the BTH Board was right and someone else was wrong – when decisions are taken that is always a risk – but I make it solely to demonstrate the influence of internal BR politics to demonstrate that they and not BTH ran Travellers-Fare.

The dilemma of the BR Board Meeting of 2nd August 1979 still remained when Messrs. Bosworth and Reid were required to review the Travellers-Fare position "in the Spring". Three reports and a strong political pressure had left nothing achieved and a meeting on 15th December 1980 to discuss "Travellers-Fare" – Its Organisational Future", noted that

"the meeting had been called to discuss the next steps necessary to place Travellers-Fare within the Board organisation when because of the privatisation initiative it needs to be separated from the BT Hotels organisations".

This was the first intimation that the BR Board was to do a complete U turn in its policy.

A paper was presented to the BR Board on 27th January 1981 with the objective of making "recommendations for the establishment of the Travellers-Fare Division of the Board". The paper contained no business or organisation argument for the change and failed to acknowledge in any way what had been achieved. It was argued that there was one principal consideration – the need to separate Travellers-Fare from BT Hotels at an early date

"so that the privatisation initiatives in respect of the latter can be developed free of restraint arising from the presence of Travellers-Fare".

Such an argument was at best misguided and, at worst, just nonsense because the greatest strength in the privatisation of BTH lay in the fact that it was not just confined to operating hotel properties and that it had a full range of catering and hotel services with which it could project itself to the market at an appropriate time. It is, of course, probable someone had already decided that Travellers-Fare presented a hindrance to the more simple route of selling the hotel properties. The paper argued the legal problems concerning the reorganisation and the authorities that are needed for it. The conclusions presented to the Board were that the presenters (Messrs. Bosworth, Reid and Burt) firmly held the view that early and complete separation of the two existing Travellers-Fare Divisions from BT Hotels was essential and that once the principle of setting up the new Division was accepted, they would then prepare appropriate proposals for bringing the Division into being. This included such things as setting terms of reference, objective and timescale for implementation

"These proposals would be submitted to the Board for approval AFTER DISCUSSION WITH THE DEPARTMENT OF TRANSPORT".

The Board were thus reducing themselves to a position where they would be influenced in their judgement by the knowledge of whether their conclusion was agreeable to the bureaucracy.

Inevitably, there emerged a Working Party to examine the detailed implications of establishing the proposed Division. This involved the time of many senior people in BTH but that mattered less. The important thing was to have a Working Party! It meant yet another distraction from the problem of running the business. It meant the end of any chance of developing the Retail and Catering Division in the High Street. The minutes of the BR Board held on 5th February 1981 that considered the paper merely mention that the paper had also been submitted to the BTH Board.

What it did not do, of course, was record to the main Board what in fact had been said at the BTH Board where the Directors had expressed their concern that they were not aware of any reasoning that led to the conclusion that Travellers-Fare should be part of BRB rather than remain part of BTH and thus become a subsidiary of British Rail Investment Limited. They believed, and were strongly wishing to record, that insufficient attention was given to their rights, duties and obligations as Directors of BTH

"It was considered also that coming at the present time when much overwork in connection with privatisation is being carried out, this proposal will add significantly to the workload".

They also expressed the view that, far from reducing overheads, the severance of the two rail catering divisions and the setting up of a BR Division would probably increase Headquarters and administrative costs.

A paper submitted to the Railways Board reporting further and in more detail on the points made when the Board held its discussions in February was produced at a March 1981 meeting. This expressed the view that there ought to be "the opportunity of upwards of a £0.5 million reduction in overheads". The truth is succinctly recorded in the Minutes of the BTH Board of 16th

July 1981 when a paper by myself and Bill Currie, the Managing Director elect of Travellers-Fare noted that the additional cost to BTH of setting up an independent Travellers-Fare Division would be £130,000 per annum and that

"accountancy methods would result in this being shown as an improvement of £375,000 in the management accounts of Travellers-Fare."

No lies were told, there was just economy in the use of the truth. If you look at one integral part of a business and ignore the whole, you will not make a proper financial judgement on the whole. The changes altered the allocation of certain costs. These allocations amounted to £505,000 of costs being carried by someone other than Travellers-Fare. The costs would not be eliminated, they would merely be re-allocated. Additional costs to be incurred in space and labour amounted to £130,000. Thus, looked at from the point of view of British Rail as a whole, there was an additional cost of £130,000 per annum. It is the truth about the part to say that overheads could be reduced by £1/2 million because they would simply not be allocated to the part and the additional costs of the part were not overheads, they were for direct labour and space.

As good loyal soldiers, the orders were carried out and, with great effort, the credit for which must in the main go to Peter Leppard, Director of Personnel, the whole separation was achieved in accordance with a predetermined programme. But, looking back, this was probably the biggest single step that resulted in the ultimate demise of BTH and probably the first capitulation of the BR Board to the bureaucracy and Politicians. There was no financial justification and certainly no sound management justification.

CHAPTER ELEVEN – THE GLENEAGLES HOTELS PLC STORY

Reference has already been made to the formation of this new company and it is necessary, in order to look at the whole story, to deal in more detail with some of the matters already recorded.

Gleneagles Hotels plc (GHP) has its beginnings in a derelict site at the back of the Caledonian Hotel in Edinburgh, a site which became the property of BTH as changes had been made over the years to the railway operations in Edinburgh. The BTH Board were faced with the problem of deciding how best to operate their resources in Edinburgh.

Edinburgh is a very important location, second only in London for the tourist business. Tourists do not necessarily want 5-star accommodation and BTH had the advantage of one of its hotels in Edinburgh being practically part of the main railway terminus. With the success in London of Grosvenor Victoria under our belt, we felt competent to approach the tourist market for Edinburgh on a similar basis. That is to say, to develop the hotel on the railway terminus as a high quality good value for money 3-star establishment in the confidence that something of the quality of the Grosvenor reproduced in Edinburgh would give us a very high share of the tourist market.

At the same time there is the fine building at the other end of Princes Street, the Caledonian Hotel which relatively recently had been enlarged by a substantial new wing with bedrooms which were good but possibly not quite in keeping with a 5-star image. At the end of Princes Street, our site was not the only one available for buildings. It adjoined a large site that was under the control of the local authority which for years had been talked about for development of civic amenities. If there was any serious thought of that being developed, it must be of advantage for the Caledonian to be developed at the same time since, to carry out our development in advance would mean living for further years on a building site while the authority developed its area. Whereas, if at best something could be done in conjunction with or at worst at the same time as, the local authority development, the whole site would be cleaned up in one go. The two star sites would be developed in close association, leading to more people being in the proximity of the hotel. Indeed, it might even be possible for those wishing to use the civic amenities to find the convenient route to them passing through the hotel. We also had to remember that, whilst for years there had been talk of the development of the Castle Hill site for hotel purposes, the fact that nothing had happened did not mean that the risk had gone away.

The BTH Board concluded early in 1980 that a satisfactory answer would be the development of the North British Hotel as a good quality 3-star unit looking for the upper middle market tourist, to give the Caledonian an appropriate face lift and develop the site in conjunction with the local authority's developments. In the threat of the possible development of the Castle Hill site, it was desirable to act with reasonable speed and the Board, seeing encouragement from a new Government to inject private sector capital into public assets, decided to tackle the financing problem.

In order to get financial backing, the Board felt that a study of the market for hotel accommodation in Edinburgh should be carried out in conjunction with a bank who may well be interested in financing the project. The Bank of Scotland was suggested and readily agreed to participate. In September 1980 the report, jointly prepared by the Bank of Scotland and British Transport Hotels was complete. It supported the Board's feelings and the strategy of involving the Bank in the work proved to be sound in that they became willing, on the security of the assets, to finance the development.

There remained the continuing indecision of the local authority and even in the absence of their commitment to develop their sites, we all felt it undesirable to invest in development of the Caledonian Hotel site beyond work to establish it firmly in the 5-star market.

Our proposals for financing with the Bank of Scotland were immediately rejected by Government and for the very first time, we learnt that their ideas on the injection of private sector money did not include borrowing from private sector against security of assets. Without that fairly usual commercial facility our field for the development of the business was rather more limited than we would have liked it to have been! Here we have the old story repeated. New Government encouraging development yet being unable to remove the dead hand of the same old Treasury rules.

We were now more than a year into a new Government who had spoken for some considerable time in opposition as people who were prepared to permit the introduction of private sector money into public sector enterprises. But, after rather more than a year of that Government, there had been no positive indication of the methods they would find acceptable nor indeed had there been any indication of any restrictions on the kind of commercial practices with which we were all familiar. When presented with an early opportunity using a very ordinary commercial practice, they found the proposal unacceptable. Here was an enterprising effort suffocated in the cradle, by negation. There were no positive ideas to follow.

This, of course, did not help the Board with its actual business problem which was to find a sum of money for the development of two hotels at either end of Princes Street. Unlike implementation of Government policies, that problem could not just wait. Our assets alone demanded we actually did something. In September 1980 in an endeavour to help the Company and, of course to ensure its own continuing interest, the Bank of Scotland invited our Deputy Chairman. Sir Alexander Glen, and myself to a lunch at which we began to explore the possibility of trying another way forward. Ideas were taken much further at a meeting at St .Pancras Chambers on 30th September when thoughts began to crystalize along the lines of putting sufficient assets together as a base and seeking to float a company that would have sufficient cash to enable the essential Edinburgh development to be carried out.

What were those assets to be? We had two glorious golfing centres in Turnberry and St Andrews. We had the legend of Gleneagles, now with four golf courses. We had the romance of the Lochalsh Hotel looking on the Isle of Skye. We had two hotels associated with the enormous tourism of Edinburgh and we had a valuable site in Edinburgh. These were all properties that offered great attraction before turning to all the business centres in Glasgow and Aberdeen and establishments in Perth and Inverness. The one major problem was that hotel business generally was not having a very good time and however we put a package together, we were compelled to show recently reducing profits and, whilst our profit performance related to earlier performances was not worse than the industry generally, it was an inescapable fact that there was a deterioration in profit, a fact that is not good when presenting oneself to the market for money, which had to be discussed if we were to go forward quickly.

In the early stages, I worked pretty well alone on the project with the representatives of the Bank of Scotland and the British Linen Bank. It was at that stage in the development the only way to work but I was receiving great support from both Sir Alexander Glen and James Forbes who were always available. In due time, a package emerged and we felt that to put together Gleneagles, the Caledonian and the North British in Edinburgh would probably be a satisfactory asset base. The package became known as Gleneagles Hotels plc.

Following detailed discussions at the BTH Board on December 12th, the Board appointed Sir Alexander Glen, our Deputy Chairman, myself, James Forbes, a non Executive Director and John Tee, our Finance Director to act as a Sub Committee of the Board with responsibility to take the matter to a formal presentation.

In outline, BTH Board agreed that there should be a holding of 45% of GHP and that an asset value of the order of £12 million should be the basis for constructing a company. The consideration of £12 million would be satisfied by BTH receiving £2.1 million cash, £4.6 million in convertible loan stock and £5.3 million in equity. The point of the convertible loan stock was to enable that investment to be transferred to equity in the event of a further equity capital raising and thus avoiding any further cash investment by the holders of the BTH shares.

It is worth pausing for a moment and recapitulating on the situation at Gleneagles. Whilst extensive maintenance was needed, the extreme could no way be argued that Gleneagles was a run-down establishment. That hotel obtained the greater part of its income from conference and group business. An arrangement existed with Bovis for the development of certain land which in our view was surplus to the Hotel requirements. This included property development and a commitment to develop more indoor leisure facilities. Such a development was sensible since existing indoor leisure facilities could then be used for extending the conference facilities of the hotel. Apart from a fairly large sum that was needed to provide decent staff accommodation, there was no major expenditure otherwise seen to be necessary at Gleneagles. People had talked about creation of leisure centres and leisure facilities with total disregard to what did in fact exist and the BTH Board always countered arguments about the need for a leisure centre at Gleneagles by asking what Gleneagles was if it was not already a centre of leisure. We did not see the need for creating great indoor sports complexes unless, of course, one were planning to open that Hotel for the whole of the year. After 50 years of operation in Perthshire, such a course seemed illogical to those who took a realistic view of the weather between November and March. Whilst the Board of BTH saw the need for capital expenditure at Gleneagles, it was more in the sense of spending to ensure the quality of service and the ambience for which it was internationally renowned and could be preserved. The major use of cash funds in the new Company was for the development in Edinburgh.

At this early stage, the size and shape of the GHP Board was being considered and it was felt that a total Board of about six with five Directors including the Chairman being Non Executive. The BTH Board felt that it would like to appoint the first Chairman for at least three years of the Company's life. It was felt that, if that could be achieved and the ongoing interest of BTH could be presented as a development and expansion of the Hotel Company then, there would be little difficulty in handling any industrial relations problems and that the staff would generally welcome any further privatisation if it could be seen in the first instance as an expansion and development of the Company they served. In our view this was also a very important point for Politicians in getting over their broad policies to have a smooth first operation.

An interim report was made to the BTH Board Meeting on 28th January by the working team. There had been one or two alterations of a relatively minor nature during the course of the close work between the British Linen Bank and ourselves. A tremendous amount of time had been taken up in these meetings but this was in no way considered time wasted. It was the first opportunity to introduce private sector finance about which we had been arguing for many years. No matter how many hours it took, it was essential to get it right and with our friends from British Linen Bank, it was a joy to work as a team with a single objective and absolute clarity of mind on how to get there.

We were, of course, misjudging the situation and, in fact, knew we were misjudging it because the one thing we could not get was any input from bureaucrats. It seemed that they had not the remotest idea what to do with the baby called privatisation and nowhere did they seem able to draw on any experience that could help them construct any guidelines to give us. It was about the time of the Board Meeting on 28th January that a letter, quite by accident, came to light which was addressed to the Director of Finance at British Railways Board from the Department of Transport and dated 15th January. This letter is signed by Mr. A. B. Brown and is headed "Escape from the Public Sector". In the normal course, pursuing the path of masterly inactivity, it would have been quite a joke, kicked into touch and kept there by many, many months of meetings and debate by which time the problem would have gone away due to changed political pressures and the file closed. In these circumstances, however, that could not be done because here was the BTH Board actually pressing to implement what it thought to be Government policy. We must have been a dreadful inconvenience! The BTH team were committed to a submission to the March 27th BTH Board Meeting. That in all would have given about six months from the first ideas to the completed project and was a pretty tight timescale in the abnormal circumstances. The bureaucrats would have to be ultimate arbitrators and for 60% of the time of the programme, they had said nothing and that does place an obstacle in the way of progress in the real world. Perhaps it wouldn't have been so bad if, when they did emerge, there had been clear thought on direction given. It is worth quoting:-

"When we had a word late last year, we briefly discussed the criteria which would have to be satisfied before any of the Board's subsidiaries into which private capital was introduced could be classified as private sector and thus freed from the financial and other constraints which Government place on nationalised industries."

This, of itself, is the introduction to a game which is about to be played with total disregard to the fortunes or otherwise of a dynamic business; to the people who, in fact, are working to try to make business a success. It acknowledges that it is Government that place financial and other constraints on classification for capital. We could remind ourselves that it is also Government that wish to grant the opportunity for private sector money. Government have created rules or accepted those created by their servants and Government have the power to direct change in those rules. However, it seems more in the interest of the bureaucrats to leave the rules as they are and devote time to discussing the criteria that has got to be satisfied within those rules in order that we can escape from them. The total difference between Government and its servants and a Board and its line management is so clear.

The document continued:

"The two basic criteria for deciding whether an economic unit is in or out of the public sector are control and ownership, in that order. This is accepted internationally in the context of national accounting although the reverse order may seem more natural."

I did not feel that BTH was going to gain a great deal from international acceptability in the context of national accounting but it was interesting to know that one of our civil servants thought the converse of the principle might be more natural. What we were more interested in was that civil servant establishing a point of view, not developing arguments around relative merits of the rules. Yet again, we find time being devoted to something that is not going to help us run or develop a profitable business one scrap.

"In broadest terms, a corporate body is regarded as in the public sector if it is both controlled and owned by Government on a basis that is intended to be permanent. Control in this context means more than the kind of control which stems from general regulatory powers. The control in question is over broad aspects of policy not day to day management: it should be clearly seen as an active form of control and not merely as a passive reserve power to be used only in time of crisis. Two relevant areas of policy are those regarding capital investment and borrowing. Pricing policy is a third area."

We were about to put to our Board a proposal that gave us substantial equity in a new company. Naturally we accepted that the remaining shareholders must have their interests properly looked after by the Board but, apparently, we, as 45% owners of equity, must not use our power as being seen to be in any kind of control over capital expenditure, financing and pricing. There cannot be many major shareholders in companies who are prevented from exercising their strength in those areas.

"Ownership may be either of the entire corporation or take the form of a dominant shareholder"

"In the context of privatisation it is important that the change in circumstances is generally accepted as being a real substance and not merely a facade. The simplest case to imagine is total disposal. The Government have no continuing liability to the buyers and place no restrictions on their actions beyond those applying to other firms in the same business. Short of total disposal the size of shareholding retained may be thought significant in relation to intentions about control. Generally speaking the smaller the residual shareholding of the Government, the easier to classify to the private sector. In any event satisfactory assurances about the withdrawal of control are necessary."

What is not made clear is who it is that needs the satisfactory assurances. This could on the one hand be seen as the Government wishing to ensure that it has even less responsibility than that of a normal shareholder. On the other hand it could be seen as a threat to the remaining shareholders that the major shareholder knows something is seriously amiss in the business and it is going to take no part in sorting it out.

"If it is decided to retain 51% or more the case for reclassification to the private sector rests solely on convincing evidence that control has been given up and that the new arrangements are intended to last. One test would be the Government's use of its voting power. Hence the announcement in the case of British Airways that the Government would not mobilise its voting power to appoint Directors and in the case of British Aerospace that whatever the precise proportion of shares that finished up in Government hands, that proportion would not in any way diminish determination not to use shareholding to exercise control. More generally the Government would have to declare the intention to stand back and leave the firm to make its own way. Moreover they would have to demonstrate by keeping back that they meant what they said for example even an implicit guarantee or borrowing would have to be avoided."

"The lack of precedence for privatisation makes it hard to draw up precise rules."

That statement sums up the dilemma perfectly. How does a Government change course if its civil servants find it difficult to draw up precise rules because there are no precedents for meeting the new Government objectives. This is probably the converse in some way of a chicken and egg argument.

"A minority shareholding by the Board in a privatised Company is not sufficient to guarantee its immunity from the public sector constraints, the burden of proof would be on the Board to demonstrate that they did not exert effective control through shareholding. I think we would want the Board to undertake that it would not use its dominant position to control policy of the company though we would, of course, accept that it could if circumstances warrant add the weight of its shareholding to the voting power of other shareholders who wishes to make changes to the Board of Directors".

Effectively that means that you are permitted to go along with others but you may not take the initiative and get others to support you.

Perhaps the masterpiece is contained in the conclusion when the writer does not

"wish to suggest that the Board will find any particular difficulty in agreeing with us the schemes which will introduce private capital into your subsidiaries and should allow them to be classified as private sector; but I thought I should perhaps draw your attention to some of the constraints which do exist so that in considering proposals for introducing private capital into parts of the Board's business you will be able to distinguish between schemes which are likely to run into trouble through the concept of symbiosis and those which are likely to be more fruitful."

Such a letter, a model of lucidity that sadly revealed the business management knowledge of the bureaucracy, in the midst of the work that was going on trying to create this new private sector enterprise had to be treated seriously and finally the BTH Working Group met Mr. Patrick Brown, the writer of the letter, and Miss Jennie Page, the Assistant Secretary, on 5th March when it was quite obvious that we were talking to superbly intelligent people who had yet to grasp an understanding of how business worked. They were, in fact, doing no more than trying to interpret instructions from the Treasury and to us, it was very sad to see such senior people not being able to apply their brains to the practical problem we were trying to solve.

At the Board Meeting on 28th January 1981, the Working Group presented their proposals. We summarised our problem in Edinburgh, drew on the conclusions of a joint report with British Linen Bank to position the North British in the 3-star market and Caledonian in the 4/5-star market. We also stated as part of our problem that we were constrained in using the normal borrowing facilities that would be available to a hotel business of our financing standing, having no charges on any of its properties we noted that our problem was not helped by a requirement from BR to provide them with £5 million from asset disposal as our share of their burden of having to live within their cash limits.

We saw as our only opportunity of the creation of a company comprising assets that BTH would wish to expand and invite cash investment in that company from private sector. We identified that this appeared to be permissible provided that BTH became a minority shareholder. The new company (GHP) would take over the three properties for a consideration of £12 million, payable to BTH by an immediate cash payment of £2 million; £5.5 million of unsecured loan stock bearing an interest rate of 6% in the first year, 7% in the second year and 8% thereafter; and £4.5 million of ordinary shares which would constitute 40% of the initial shareholding in GHP. The 60% balance remaining of the share capital would be made available to interested investors for a cash consideration of £6.75 million which, subject to the £2 million cash paid to BTH would all be available to the new company.

We then outlined how, in our view, the cash could be used by the new company and this was:-

1.   To close the North British Hotel, Edinburgh for approximately nine months while it was altered to increase the number of bedrooms from 200 to 231 and at the same restructured organisationally to respond to a 3-star status. The market it would then seek was one that would produce high volume at a modest charge.

2.   At the same time, the Caledonian would be upgraded to 4/5 star standing to concentrate on the luxury market.

3.   Gleneagles to be refurbished to reinforce its 5-star status specifically providing for improved conference facilities.

It was seen that those three items together with certain elements of renewal and refurbishments could involve a total expenditure of approximately £7 million over three years and so far as cash was required over and above that provided by the initial flotation, it would be provided out of earnings in the first three years with the new group showing a positive cash flow of some significance from year 4.

These proposals were fully supported by our advisers, British Linen Bank, who were of the opinion that investors would respond positively to the proposal.

One of the most significant points about the proposal was that we were able to demonstrate that the investment retained by BTH plus the earnings on the cash portion of the consideration would result in the total earnings to BTH exceeding those they had earned in operating the hotels over recent years. Additionally, BTH would have a 40% share in the equity which, of itself, should, subject to the success of the company, increase in value. This, we saw as a considerable distraction from the inevitable arguments that would emerge about the amount of discount below valuation at which the property was put into the new company. It really was very relevant in the proposal to understand that we were going to earn more than we had earned owning the entire property and still retain a 40% interest in any growth that took place in the company. By any standards within the constraints that had been placed upon the company, it was a proposal to be recommended.

However, the Working Group were all men who had spent a considerable part of their lives in the private sector and, shortly after the agreement of their proposals by the BTH Board, they sought the advise of Peat, Marwick, Mitchell & Co. to establish that the constraints under which they had been placed by the Department and Treasury had cost the state a considerable sum of money and the alternative they favoured would have been financially beneficial. On 27th March, they reported to the BTH Board that if BTH had been allowed to operate in the circumstances of other hotel groups, they would have had no difficulty in raising loan finance either to build a new hotel in Edinburgh or for the North British conversion because the company, with no attaching mortgages to its property, was in an usually favourable position as a borrower. Because its single source of capital was BR, it was, by rules established by the Treasury, linked to the public sector borrowing requirements and thus any problems British Rail might have in financing its main business. They pointed out the lack of clarity in the way the Government wished to implement what was generically now known as privatisation and whilst the options range from simple disposal to individual partnerships, there is no clarity on the extent to which BTH may participate in a partnership beyond saying that control must pass from BTH.

The document prepared for the team by Peat, Marwick, Mitchell & Co. demonstrated that following the completion of the essential investment programme financed in the normal way with BTH remaining sole shareholders, that a profit of £2.5 million per annum would be earned and, that by financing on the method required by Government policy, £1.24 million per annum less would be earned, to which must: be added the penalty of only having the 40% share in the increasing value of the assets. A very high price to pay for the constraints of political ideology and the non-commercial method of its implementation.

The Board, or more particularly the Non Executive Directors (who were in spite of their non-executive status doing a considerable amount of work on the privatisation front) were particularly critical and expressed extremely strong views at the Board Meeting on 27th March. After nearly six months of work, we had submitted our first privatisation proposal. We had been severely handicapped by lack of information from bureaucrats and, towards the end of putting the project together, we were further interrupted by the insistence of the staff of the newly formed British Rail Investments Limited flexing its muscles.

At the Board, Sir Alexander Glen drew attention to the consequences on the Board's business of the various changes in policy over the preceding year which was emphasised in its effects by the rapidly growing recession in the UK. From a position two or three years ago where there was a reasonable and respected hotel business, BTH was now dispirited and declining. Following the policy laid down early in 1978, great effort had been put into developing a free standing business when we were now being told that assets should be sold to help meet railway losses. Privatisation was increasingly a vast obscurity of real meaning with threat of sale by tender. In these circumstances, it is perhaps not surprising that the senior line management is distracted. Sir Alexander Glen asked that the Board should be in no doubt that the hotel part of their business was running downhill and that despite great efforts, results were deteriorating and, that unless policy could be clarified as to where we wished to go, the eventual cost was likely to be disastrous.

GPH had been chosen as the first serious attempt at privatisation. We had worked well with our advisers who must have begun to doubt our purpose. Government instructed us to go down this road to privatisation and the BRB to do so in a way least unacceptable to the Unions. GHP would certainly seem nearer both objectives that any outright sale. We were now told time would be needed to convince the civil servants. It was the Government that set us on this road and if they could not make up their own minds, Sir Alexander submitted, it was for the Board to go direct to the Secretary of State.

Finally, Sir Alexander drew attention to the excessive burden which senior executives and non executives alike were carrying; whilst he believed that the opportunity for building a new base for profitable operation of BT Hotels could still be achieved and he had no intention of withdrawing from that attempt, at the same time, he was convinced that the time had come for unambiguous speech.

The proposals were looked at by BRIL and also by Morgan Grenfell, the BR Board's merchant bankers, and by the Department of Transport, whose advisers were also Morgan Grenfell. At the British Railways Board on 2nd April, the only variation to the proposal was suggested by BRIL in the form that more cash payment should be received with a reduction in the loan stock held in the new company. It was noted that the proposal would meet Trade Union aspirations but that care must be taken that precedents were not set for any future propositions. Morgan Grenfell apparently drew attention to the problems of any large though minority equity holder and emphasised the importance of ensuring that the profits forecast were reliable. The British Railways Board approved the project in principle, subject to the detailed arrangements being submitted for formal ratification by the Board when BRIL had accepted and the necessary approval had been obtained from the Department of Transport and Treasury.

From this moment, the whole matter was out of the control of the BTH Board.

It is interesting to note that, in their comments, Morgan Grenfell on the 30th March 1981 concluded that they could not help having the feeling that

"this project is under consideration for all the wrong reasons although this is clearly a commercial decision on your part and I fully understand most of your thinking which has led to this decision".

Presumably their advice to the Department would have been the same!

By the end of May the proposal approved by the BTH Board had, as a result of discussion between BRIL and the Department, changed considerably. The nominal loan stock had been reduced from £5.5 million to £1.5 million with an increase in the cash taken from £2 million to £5.75 million. The immediate cash was to be £3 million with two equal payments after one and two years on the balance. Shareholding was to be reduced to one-third. The Working Group reported back to the BTH Board on these proposals saying that the reduced equity holding and the reduction in the loan stock could leave the Board in a more difficult situation since outside parties could make a bid more easily for the institutional equity holdings or for an individual hotel a short time from the deal being concluded. They repeated their view that the 27th March proposal had embodied a sensible degree of continuity, particularly as it affected staff employment but that the new proposal should not seriously affect that objective. They also noted that underlying the proposal was an understanding that each hotel would be developed much along the line planned by BTH although GHP must reserve to itself the final decision. There had been no change of view in the development plan but the fact that BTH's equity stake had been so subsequently reduced made us feel that the Board should be given a greater assurance on the ongoing use and development of the assets and protection in the medium term against outside events that did not basically form part of the proposed arrangements; events which it would be impossible for the BTH to stop since it would be required to give undertakings not to use its strength to control. The Working Group reminded the BTH Board that their objective was to raise sufficient money to enable essential changes to be made to the North British Hotel,

Edinburgh and that piecemeal, this had been relegated in importance as the interpretation of Government policy was invented. By now it must be noted that BTH were required to surrender two-thirds of their equity interest in Gleneagles and the Edinburgh Hotel without being so sure of achieving its original objective. On the other hand, British Rail received an additional £3.75 million, the future use of which was to say the least, doubtful.

On 15th May, the British Railways Board formally sought the approval of the Department of Transport for the proposals. The whole matter then moved into the Political arena; the steps in which are quite fascinating.

On 15th May when final submission was made to the Department of Transport, I think we all heaved a sigh of relief that the job was over but, we misjudged the situation rather badly because of our continued belief that we were involved in a commercial decision. We did not find the interference of British Rail Investments Limited either helpful or constructive but we settled our differences amicably and accepted that they had to make the final decision even though it was not necessarily as we would have done it. We could see the Political pressure on them and, in all fairness, they were chosen for it and had to be more accommodating than we would be.

In submitting the proposals, we gave a timetable that required the issue of the proposals on 26th May; a visit to be arranged with prospective investors on 3rd June to each of the hotels; application forms to be sent to the prospective investors for return by 18th June; with completion of the transaction on 22nd June. This timetable was established by British Linen Bank as being fairly fast but reasonable. There was no point in delaying the implementation of the decision that had been reached unless one felt there would be considerable doubt in convincing investors that the proposition was good. Whilst the Bank had expressed reservations that the 27th March proposal had been made less attractive to the investors as a result of the Departmental accommodation, they did not at any time feel that the placing would fail.

In response to the submission, the officials indicated that the Secretary of State, Mr. Norman Fowler, personally wanted to have a presentation made to him and that this could not take place before he returned from Helsinki on Monday 1st June when, provided all his questions were satisfactorily answered, it was hoped that the Secretary of State would give approval fairly quickly after the presentation. It was said that he would wish to have the rationale of taking the course of selecting only three hotels explained and to hear some part of the philosophy to deal with the balance of the hotels and other businesses in BTH. The rationale had been fully explained in the memorandum of 15th May but not, of course, anything concerning the remainder of the hotels. A particularly important point to note when later we shall see how he defended his action when questioned in the House. The last point they made was the real hint of trouble to come when they wished to have explained to them the reasoning for the discount that had arisen between the valuation and the consideration in the Placing Document. Clearly, the questions had been devised and fed to him by the Civil Servants. It would be unusual for a politician to have sufficient command of the subject to frame his own questions but the tragedy was that there was no-one in our experience over the last six months capable of making a commercial judgement, let alone framing really searching questions. This was a case where the Secretary of State would probably have got more by talking to us without "Sir Humphrey".

Managerially, we had the very delicate problem of consulting as part of the normal process with the Trade Unions on these proposals and, before we took that step, we really wanted to be sure our pitch was not going to be queered at the political level. A paper was prepared for each of the Trade Unions and informal discussions took place. Whilst the NUR did not like the idea on a political basis, they were very quick to see the advantage on a business basis. They saw an opportunity for themselves as a Trade Union to become one of the investors. They saw that the livelihoods of their members was being protected and they saw the realisation of funds which could be available for the development of the remainder of the group. Our dealings with the Transport Salaried Staff Association were not quite so successful, primarily because we were quite unable to get an acceptance that we could speak with the Trade Union leaders about what was going to emerge and still keep it as a private discussion. There was, at that time, a slightly unfortunate attitude prevailing in their Union hierarchy that demanded that they should exercise their freedom to make everything public and it was not helpful when the whole of the discussion was immediately published in their Trade Union journal.

The evening of 1st June saw our team present themselves to the Secretary of State, heavily flanked on both sides by his civil servants.

There were no questions of any particular difficulty raised and the pure business aspect of the proposals seemed to be of little interest with the Secretary of State being concerned with the difficulties he might have in dealing with Trade Union reaction; how he could defend the price against a valuation and how he could anticipate questions that would be asked in the House. Slowly I began to realise that I wasn't at a business meeting at all.

The time available was handled brilliantly. We knew the time the Secretary of State would be standing up to announce that he had to go to the House, and that time was rapidly approaching and we were still no nearer to getting a reaction on the business proposals. With immaculate timing and about five minutes to go, the Secretary of State delivered his verdict. He pointed out that there was no need for him to authorise the business proposal at all and that all the law required was for him to authorise British Rail to take shares in a new company. He said that he had examined the format for the new company and was satisfied that British Rail could own shares in it but it was then a matter entirely for British Rail management as to whether it sold its assets into that company and was no concern of his. The tables were completely turned in one stroke so as to leave the BR Chairman apparently free to make his decision. Since January, those of us working to put this project together had put up with nothing but useless business dialogue from his Departmental officials who, we were now told, were apparently only concerned with whether BR could invest in the new company. Two days later in the House, the Secretary of State answered a question by Mr. Cowans, saying that the proceeds of the sale would go to the owners , the British Railways Board.

"Part of the purpose of the sale is to enable the Board to use the money to invest further in the hotel business".

This was perhaps the hardest pill of all to swallow, against a requirement set to BTH to provide £5 million to BR from sale of assets to meet its external financing limits.

The format of the first attempt by the Department to indicate the Secretary of State's agreement makes interesting reading.

"I can now let you know that on the material available to him at present the Secretary of State will in principle be ready to issue his formal consent to the acquisition of the shares at the appropriate time."

This was of no value as an authority since a Placing Document was about to be issued in which BTH committed themselves to take one-third of the equity capital. So the letters continued to flow until officially, on 15th June, formal consent was given to the acquisition of the shares in Gleneagles Hotels plc.

When the appropriate time came for the investors to take their opportunity, money was not all that readily forthcoming. Much has been said about this being a company with Scottish money, even if such money could be defined there was not a lot of it about when the time for investment came. Indeed, it would not be unfair to say that the barrel had to be scraped pretty hard to get the final funds and private investors were accepted in order to ensure the issue was a success.

In the months that followed, as the new management took its place, I was obliged to keep silent, as the former management of BTH was frequently attacked. The habit tended to establish itself and even several years after the event when one is perfectly free to speak, I find it less than worthy to respond. For those who wish to check, the facts are there for everyone to see. In the Placing Document, the profit performance under BTH management is set out in Appendix 11. It is quite a simple arithmetic exercise to apply an inflation factor to those profit achievements and see how well the company is doing against the performance of the BTH management it was so willing to criticise. The new Managing Director was indeed a very lucky young man to be head-hunted into a company that had been formed by the very management he subsequently chose to attack at every opportunity and which presented him with a balance sheet with £5 million of cash ready to spend to develop the company. Not many young executives can start a new job with that kind of advantage but that is exactly what the BTH management team set out to do. The only difference is that they were of a mind that they would actually be allowed to enjoy developing the Company but politics deemed otherwise.

CHAPTER TWELVE – OTHER
PRIVITISATION PROGRESS

Whilst in 1981, the Gleneagles project was our single biggest privatisation achievement to date, there were many others which had they been allowed to be brought to fruition, would have dealt with a much larger proportion of the Company. Apart from one project, the others were individually smaller and were not as well advanced as the Gleneagles discussions when British Rail Investments Limited began to get involved. It had power but no clear directive, strategy or tactics – a danger in the adolescent! There were many stresses beginning to show. The BTH Board had four Members with real practical business experience to whom the problem of the introduction of private sector cash, far from representing any insurmountable problem, was seen as a straightforward opportunity not to be missed. But, of course, they had the disadvantage of being motivated by commercial considerations. The Chairman of the BTH Board was in certain difficulties because he could not ignore the political pressures that were being brought directly and indirectly on BR since he was its Deputy Chairman. This was not a natural or easy role for him because he too, at heart, had an entrepreneurial, commercial approach to dealing with the developments. The strong business attitude of the BTH Board had to be controlled. It was rather uncomfortable for the career railway members of the Board who, by their experience, had grown to live with a political and bureaucratic interference that was unacceptable to a commercial organisation. The way the BTH handled its business was indeed a breath of fresh air to them and I think they enjoyed it is a cautious way. The BTH Board relied on its authority now being delegated from British Rail Investments Limited, no longer from the BR Board, and very soon its authority to act by itself in any matter of privatisation was withdrawn. Perhaps this was predictable after the Board committed the unforgivable sin on 28th January 1981 when the non executive directors expressed concern at not being aware of the reasoning for the decision for the segregation of Travellers-Fare from BTH. They did not actually believe that the Board ran the company and that their role was to reason why, rather than just to do and die.

There were several clear pressures which were not leading in the same general direction.

There was the political pressure to implement that dogma which was placed on the BR Board. It was an ideology, a dogma without a thought as to method of implementation and until those who were anxious to implement it came forward with some proposal, there was absolutely nothing by way of constructive guidance given politically. The policy formers were entirely reactive in matters of implementation, seeing only one course that could provide the protection they needed in any decision taken.

The total lack of experience in dealing with business matters on the part of civil servants led them to see the only safe route as being that of outright sale by public auction. They had no idea how to justify, even to themselves let alone their political masters, a negotiated sale as an acceptable result.

British Rail Investments Limited were in a dilemma. On one hand, they did not want to set themselves up as a large centralised staff but, on the other, how could they be effective without some staffing. They helped solve this by having consultants seconded to them. With the best will in the world, there is no way that a young professional, seconded for one year, can get sufficient understanding of the business to make constructive proposals for its development. It is fine if their role is to be akin to that of a receiver but, to our joy, the Secretary of State had talked in terms of developing the business.

The BTH Board was most anxious to use the political initiative but only when it made good commercial sense.

Keeping some sort of balance with all of those interests was of itself a full time job for me but there was still a company to run and a number of opportunities to be evaluated, considered and then implemented. How one longed for the simple disciplines of the private sector and avoidance of the nonsense arising from too many people, each with power that could not be ignored, protecting their flanks.

The general state of the equipment in the laundering and dry cleaning part of the business had, for some time, been the cause for concern. Probably the decision to have these establishments was correct at the time it was taken but, many years later, following technical developments that had taken place in the laundry and dry cleaning industry as a whole, it was questionable. Without substantial investment it was unlikely that we could compete with the service quality that could be provided by normal commercial laundries.

Discussions with the Sunlight Services Group led us to a conclusion that we should sell all of our business to them, together with the whole stock of linen and we should move to a contract hire arrangement for future supply. The Board saw the proposition as good in financial terms and acknowledged the delicacy with which industrial relations would have to be handled. The matter had been discussed with our professional banking advisers who were of the opinion that the proposals represented a good deal for the company and that there was little purpose in trying to negotiate with other potential purchasers. The deal included adequate protection for BRB Laundry and dry cleaning services. The Board's nervousness concerning industrial relations problems was quite rightly expressed, since this was the first outright sale to a private sector investor. But, in the negotiations, proper care had been taken to ensure that the two laundries in York and Edinburgh would have some guarantee as to being kept open.

British Rail Investments Limited insisted that there should be more investigation. This was done and time went by and eventually, many months later, a deal was put together that was little better than the original proposals and certainly no better after considering the many months of benefit that were lost, the management time that was involved and the effect on the people who by now knew they were up for sale.

At the beginning of 1981, we were approached by the owners of the Clarendon Hotel in Derby as to our intentions regarding the Midland Hotel in the City. The Midland Hotel had given us cause for concern for many years and for many reasons that were outside of our control. As the City had developed, the Hotel, which for many years stood in an area that could best be described as a large building site, was too far away from the centre. The lack of investment in the hotel could, to some extent be justified by its business performance but it would be unforgivable to let it just drift on. In the Clarendon Hotel, a young entrepreneurial hotelier was in charge and seemed to have created the kind of hotel that was needed. It offered a good restaurant and bar and bedroom quality that matched the requirement of the business traveller to the City. Whilst the grand railway hotel image of yesteryear that had once been the style of the first railway hotel in the world was clearly not the style that was needed anymore in Derby. It was questionable whether BR had the managerial skills to move into the less affluent market. It soon became clear in the discussions that it would be sensible to try to embrace the Royal Victoria Hotel, Sheffield, into the same deal, since here again was a hotel with practically the same problem as that facing the Midland Hotel, Derby. Discussions progressed well and, by 22nd April 1981, the BTH Board agreed the proposal subject to a couple of small changes in the financing which I was able to report to the meeting of the Board on 21st May as having been agreed. So far, so good, but of course, the BTH Board had to obtain the authority of BRIL who had to obtain the authority of civil servants who, in turn had to seek the approval of the Treasury who would be concerned that we were to retain 40% equity in the business with the fear that it might not, therefore, be excluded from public sector borrowing.

The deal was finally completed in April 1982. We were extremely lucky to be able to hold the partners together for the whole of that time but in that one deal alone every lesson on privatisation was learned and I think we all fully understood why nothing concerned with politicians or bureaucracy should be involved in ownership of a commercially competitive business. It took approximately three months to put the deal together and it then took practically a year to get it approved and implemented. The important commercial point was that here were two BTH hotels that were ready for development in a manner in which the BTH management did not have the skill. By putting them together with a management that did possess that skill, there was a promising new business for development. That was the objective with which we started and the objective we finally achieved. But what a route to realise half a million pounds.

The Old Course Hotel at St. Andrews was already heavily publicised as the only hotel BTH had acquired in fifty years. It happened to be true but it was also one of the biggest embarrassments in the portfolio so far as ability to earn profit was concerned. In its existing form, just about everything was wrong with it apart from its beautiful situation. It was a new hotel but designed to meet the classical BTH style. The hotel situated in its position is fairly obviously designed to cater for golfing holidays. Successful golfing holidays often demand two things; first that the residents should actually have a right to play golf; and second that the golfing widows do not become miserable. There were no rights by the hotel to play golf on the public courses at St. Andrews and there was practically nothing to do if you were not actually playing golf. In our view, to get it right as a hotel, it had to follow the lines of becoming a hotel and country club with many leisure facilities. But even then the disadvantage that there was no way in which guests could have a right to play on the most famous courses in the world remained. In our judgement, it was necessary to spend many hundreds of thousands of pounds to achieve the product objective; a very spectacular venture.

We examined very thoroughly the possibility of converting the property into self-contained units of different sizes for development on a timeshare basis. Three months were spent preparing a study which clearly had many attractions. To implement it would mean a serious deflection of management attention from all the other matters that were then in the pipeline.

This could have been a very great challenge to the company management and in all the circumstances, it was the right decision not to proceed at that time.

As was the case with many properties, there was a constant flow of people wanting to buy them, provided they were at jumble sale prices and St. Andrews was no exception. Quite out of blue, a serious buyer appeared and immediately talked in terms of cash prices that had to be listened to. The ideas that were outlined by Mr. Frank Sheridan were similar but more ambitious than those we had considered ourselves but my principle concern was that he was clearly a man who was not prepared to hang about putting up with the layers of treacle through which we had to pass before a decision could be implemented. Fairly quickly, we agreed on a price around one and a quarter million pounds which was very roughly double the value placed on the property by Christies and about four times the book value. I had little difficulty convincing the Board and, in a remarkable time of about three months, we managed to complete the deal. From an industrial relations viewpoint this did in fact turn out to be a godsend in timing since the hotel was closed for the winter with only a dozen staff retained. That soothed the nerves of the bureaucrats. It was a nice simple sale in which they were able to protect their Minister from any accusations of selling below the market value. The whole thing occurred so quickly by their standards that their principle concern was in establishing that I had no personal connection with Mr. Frank Sheridan as a result of which perhaps I might in some way benefit.

At Moretonhampstead, there was a stable block situated in a beautiful position on the golf course and adjoining the drive up to the hotel. Whilst a very small part of this building was used for residential purposes and storage of groundsmen's equipment, in the main it was falling into ruin and, in our view, formed a good location for a timeshare development. Half a dozen or so developers were invited to show an interest and three responded. Following their presentations, we decided on the most acceptable. By November 1981, we had agreed with the DFDS for the site to be leased for 80 years for £190,000 with a contribution of up to £35,000 towards the building of a swimming pool in the Hotel complex. The management company to run the timeshare would pay £3,000 per annum for the upkeep of roads and each timeshare owner was granted two green fees per day on the course with the use of any other leisure facilities in the Hotel on the same basis as they could be used by any hotel guest. A very good commercial deal was thus put together that could enable something of the order of a quarter of a million pounds to be spent to complete the development of the Manor House Hotel.

We did press as a prerequisite that a quick decision could be given so that the first timeshare property could be available for the beginning of the 1982 season which was something like five months away. To take this to a conclusion, we had to have someone from headquarters to help. Perhaps it was to keep an eye on us because we certainly were not aware of our need for assistance. What should have been a simple matter between each of the company's respective surveyors and legal advisers became progressively more and more of a nightmare because our development proposal was clearly a thorn in the side of anyone who was making his prinicipal objective a clean sale of the business. A deadline was finally set by DFDS to exchange contracts on 30th July 1982, eight months after setting up the deal and a date which clearly missed the objective of having a timeshare available for the 1982 season but, even then at the eleventh hour "experts" were still arguing about the length of time we had committed any subsequent owner to provide golf on the premises. Sir Alexander Glen, the Deputy Chairman, who had given such a great support to the line management throughout the whole of this period, suggested that if he as Deputy Chairman and myself as Managing Director were satisfied that we had fulfilled the requirements that the BTH Board had specified then we were free to sign the agreement. We had been perfectly happy for several months on that score but we checked again to be certain. Without further reference we signed the agreement with DFDS and then collected the flack that followed from BRIL. All told, that deal, which involved less than £200,000 took practically one year from inviting people to consider the idea through to implementation.

Whilst Sir Alexander and I had to take a severe reprimand from Mike Bosworth, we were all smiling to ourselves at a very interesting legal position had things become really rough. Our protection was that BTH was a registered company and, as such, the responsibility for its management was with its directors. We merely acted in accordance with their decision and therefore could not be faulted. Good fun, but we were not kidding ourselves, we know the score.

There were two disappointing failures during this time. One concerned the wine business and the other the possibility of a partnership with another major hotel group.

As far back as 1979, we had identified problems with our wine business. The old railway hotels and the famous St. Pancras Cellars had enormous reputation and tradition for the quality of wine. As wine had become more popular, a new generation of buyers, sellers and indeed consumers had emerged. In Clive Coates, we had a Master of Wine who was held in the highest esteem in the trade. There is no doubt we had acquired a wonderful stock and there is equally no doubt that as a business proposition we had got a disaster.

We needed more outlets than the hotels and there had been, over a short time, a very well developed mail order business in the form of the Malmaison Wine Club. This had the excellent reputation to which it was entitled since there was no other mail order business backed up by such a fine range of stock.

We planned and implemented our move into the wholesale business but our greatest need was to get retail outlets in the High Street and the one thing that BTH was forbidden by law to do was operate in the High Street. We therefore began to look for partners and before long, we seemed to be attracting very many prospective partners ranging from seedy nightclub owners to reputable traders but very few people without a cash flow problem. When we disclosed the level of our capital investment, they all ran away. In the meantime we were pursuing a ruthless stock cutting programme and the totally unheard of situation of BTH not actually buying wine for a year became a reality. It was a great pity that we couldn't put something together that would have preserved the great quality that had been achieved under the direction of Clive Coate's predecessor but, unfortunately, our ambition outstripped our self financing ability.

By far and away the biggest disappointment was the failure to put together a joint company with De Vere. Over many years the development of that fine group of hotels had been observed. It was felt that there was a market similarity in the quality objectives of De Vere and BTH. It was a most pleasant surprise when, through mutual friends, we were able to get together to talk and it was most encouraging to see that both sides could see the value of a large organisation that brought together the best of both companies. At about the time of our discussions with De Vere, we were also having many discussions with the Reo Stakis organisation where again there was some compatibility with certain of our units. We had built up under Sir Alexander Glen's leadership for BTH and Mr Leslie Jackson's leadership for De Vere, an excellent relationship by the middle of 1981 that we were confident could be taken to a very satisfactory conclusion.

Suddenly we found ourselves subjected to a BRIL Board 'strategy', constructed before considering the plan that they had called on BTH to produce. This strategy was announced as being to sell certain hotels and to continue to operate a limited number. What BTH could do in about three years with those would be compared with the sort of deal that could be made with an outside private party now. BRIL saw De Vere as one of the possible outside parties. Such a strategy is quite unbelievable. To think that an organisation of the quality and standing of De Vere would be prepared to continue talking to someone who wanted to sell the best units, continue to operate some because they had got difficult railway connections in a property sense and from the rag bag that was left consider joining forces. Such philosophy could only emerge from the experts seconded to BRIL for a year. It is straight out of the toy cupboard text book and totally lacking any understanding of the industry and the people in it.

The meetings that we were directed to continue to have with De Vere took place and it was not at all surprising that Leslie Jackson made his position very clear to the consultant advising BRIL on their strategy and who now had to accompany us at any of our meetings. I could only describe my own feelings as being livid that months of work that were leading to an exceptionally good commercial arrangement were ruined by the attitude of people who had not even taken the trouble to try to understand what was being put together but felt themselves able to pontificate to men of stature and achievement that exceeded their wildest expectation from life.

Perhaps it was unfortunate that experience elsewhere and in BR gave me some sympathetic understanding of the problems that BR were trying to handle. They were being leaned on politically and were being led to believe that approval of their railway investments may be linked to their progress in the disposal of their subsidiary businesses to meet a political ideology. Alas, also they were not the favourite sons of our leading political figures.

CHAPTER THIRTEEN – THE BTH
PROPOSALS TO BRIL

In September 1981, the BTH Board agreed its Business Plan for submission to British Rail Investments Limited.

The objectives of British Railways Board in introducing private capital into its businesses are summarised in the Chairman's Commentary on the BR Annual Report and Accounts 1980:

"As long ago as 1977 I urged that we should examine the possibilities of joint venture capital leading to further opportunities to develop our subsidiary businesses. For too long their growth has been stunted for lack of resources inhibited by the constraints of the public sector borrowing requirements.

"The Board will be maintaining a significant interest in these businesses which grew out of railway activities.

"What the Board of BR seeks from this new legislation is scope for introducing investment which should improve the cash flows of BR in due course from its businesses and also widen the opportunities for those who work in them."

In May 1981 the remit of British Rail Investments Limited was established and in constructing our plan we summarised that remit and noted the way we saw it applying to BTH, as follow:-

1.　　To ensure that the business passes as soon as practicable into majority private sector ownership and into effective private sector control. We reminded our principals that we had already achieved a substantial step in this direction with the Gleneagles/Edinburgh project and with the Derby/ Sheffield project.

2.　　To enable the business to expand and develop. Here we noted that we interpreted this to mean that the extinction of the Company was not envisaged and that plans should aim to establish a sound base for future expansion in the private sector.

3.　　To remove the business from any public sector controls on borrowing, investment, etc. which may in the past have inhibited performance and growth. We had in mind here the many hoops through which we had had to pass in setting up the Gleneagles Company to meet the accountancy aspirations of the Treasury.

4.　　To ensure that proper commercial benefits are obtained from the disposal of assets and surrender of future income prospects. Here we noted that there could be a conflict between meeting this objective and pressure to make early progress to achieve political objectives.

5.　　To maintain a significant interest in the business and influence over its affairs by, for example, retaining shareholding or keeping the right to nominate directors. Here we wished to register our view that shareholders' responsibilities are defined and that regardless of who those shareholders are, they should live by the law which is established with regard to shareholders rights.

6.　　To have full regard to the interests of the Company's staff and to widen the opportunities open to them. We noted that our interpretation of that objective was that the large scale sacking of people was not an objective, nor were the terms and conditions of employment a principal area for attack.

7.　　To enable that the preliminary activity of BRB, i.e. operating the Railway, is not affected adversely.

The Board then stated its primary responsibilities as being:-

1.   To remunerate the capital employed in and to develop the business of hotels and accommodation, preserving the fabric of the properties.

2.   To generate sufficient cash from the operations to provide for replacement of resources (except for property) and for minor development.

3.   Providing expanding career opportunities for employees at all levels.

The Business Plan set out seven options that had been considered and then argued each of these options against the BRIL remit and the Company's interpretation of it which was not challenged. The recommended option proposed the disposal of failed assets, the use of funds to develop sound assets, a programme that would in two years establish a sound profit position, the contraction of Company administration in line with the established programme of devolution of control and continued moves for partnerships with the private sector. Financially, the Company would be self sufficient over the period 1982 to 1984. We had an excellent record of living within cash flow forecasts over the past two years and there was no justification whatsoever for doubting our proposals on that score. There was no cash required from British Rail Investments Limited or BR and in no way could the Plan or indeed the past two years be described in words that inferred that BTH was any financial drain or embarrassment to BR.

The Plan proposed a cash contribution to BRIL of £5 million over the three years. At the end of that time, BRIL could expect a cash flow of the order of £4 million per annum which it could either retain for itself, and the benefit of BR, by continuing with the ownership of the Company, or alternatively have a sound base upon which a flotation would be possible.

The BTH Board, in their Plan, were anxious that their masters should understand that we were not involved in a kind of glorious case study; there was a large business to run and, with changes in objective, bad communication regarding objectives and the diversion of line management, they were concerned that the management team could not properly carry out its duties.

The Board were right in expressing these views and, as the Chief Executive, I was very pleased to know their concern and appreciated their support. At the same time, I was not all that worried about the line management. Whilst I would have liked to have had more time to direct and influence it, we were in the advantageous position of the new organisation structure working extremely well and we had three good Executive Directors – Dennis Aldridge, Derek Plant and Harry Hyde – with supporting teams who were doing a good job in running the operations. In John Tee we had a sound Finance Director and Christopher Dunn was building a good Sales and Marketing team. The position could have been very much worse and, whilst the Board appreciated the great effort of my management team, they could see that the pressures on us were quite unreasonable, outside of their control and as human beings, we would crack one day. Happily there were no signs of it.

In presenting the Plan, the Board took the opportunity of reminding BRIL of the need for creative and compatible relationships. We all understood the pressures that were being brought to bear on BR and BRIL by the politicians and bureaucrats but, at the same time, we were very strong in holding our ground that, as Directors of the Company, our duties were given to us by Company legislation not by politicians. There is little doubt that we were always at risk of a head-on collision course since our single objective was the good commercial development of the assets and people in British Transport Hotels. Given time, collision could be avoided by management of politicians and their bureaucrats. More than once, I was told that that was not the role of the BTH Board or, my management team. There were others responsible for that relationship.

Our Plan did not anticipate some great improvements in the economic climate or any easy way to higher earnings. The hotel business in Great Britain was very depressed and had been so for two years. We knew that we had now taken all the actions on the cost front to ensure financial success from much lower volume of business than had been achieved in the halcyon days of 1977. We wished it to be noted that the BTH Board had demonstrated its ability to bring about privatisation, to manage its cost structure and, particularly, to control its cash flow. We wished to restate our commitment to getting out of the public sector in a considered and disciplined manner, not in a haphazard one, to meet some political ideology. Our message was that we wished to trade our assets at the right moment, at the right price and from a position of strength.

On 2nd October, Sir Alexander Glen and I, on behalf of the Board, presented ourselves to the British Rail Investments Limited Board to discuss the Plan. The meeting was very disappointing in that we were to be allowed one hour to make the presentation and for discussion. Feeling that our document had been clearly presented and assuming it had been read, we concentrated on identifying five major points.

The first was to reiterate our enthusiasm to take the chance that was now before us. This Company had not been encouraged to show any business initiative for 20 years and we were in the wonderful position of having sorted out most of our excessive cost problems; had got a clear view of where we should take the Company and, over the past two years, had got a pretty good management performance measured in terms of cost control, product rationalisation and control of cash flow.

Our second point was that we had been no drain on BR cash resources over the last three years but that our investment allowance had mainly been used to meet fire precaution requirements, renewals and redecoration.

The third point was to plead for stability, pointing out that in 1979 we had agreed a strategy with BR Board which, by the end of 1980, was cancelled. No management of a commercial enterprise can possibly live in that kind of situation.

Our fourth point was that at the same time, we must not be tied to a blue print drawn to satisfy Treasury rules and commercially disoriented Departmental officials. We must have a broad directional strategy within which we retained flexibility to take advantage of business opportunities as they arose. We had in mind the recent experiences that have been recorded in the previous chapter, where the timescale for decision taking was reasonable up to the point of the BTH Board and thereafter totally unacceptable by any business standards. We were not foolish enough to argue for absolute power but we were strong in arguing that we didn't want a very long and strait jacket.

Out fifth point was to re-emphasise the need for a strategy consistent with good business principles so that even while we were working in the public sector, we could be strengthening ourselves for the time when we would be free of all political and bureaucratic shackles and enjoy the freedom and ease of private sector.

The meeting was unfortunately short but we felt that we had been warmly received by the BRIL Directors and that they understood our case. The next stage was for BRIL to submit a document to the meeting of the British Railways Board on 5th November and it was then that the gulf that existed between BRIL's intentions and the BTH Board's Plan appeared. The BR Board were told that the BRIL Board, as early as 30th June, had considered the various options for privatisation and agreed which hotels should be disposed of in any event and others where there might be problems concerning commercial leases from the BR Board and which might, therefore, have to be retained; that the remainder of the hotels might either be retained for improvement and subsequent disposal provided BTH could demonstrate the financial advantages of doing so, or might otherwise be disposed of more quickly to private sector interests. There was no relationship between the draft report to the BR Board and the meeting of 2nd October.

Another very important point emerged which, so far as the Company was concerned, appeared for the first time. It was in regard to the BRIL remit where the first objective recorded earlier in this chapter is amended to read

"to ensure that the business passes as soon as practicable – and certainly within the life of this parliament – into majority private sector ownership and into active private sector control".

It is extremely difficult to understand how good commercial interest can be reconciled with the life of a parliament. After studying the draft submission to the BR Board, there really was quite a rumpus, not the least from some members of British Rail Investments Limited Board. By the time the Minutes of the BR Board meeting became available, it again became clear that there was some influence being brought to bear other than the consideration by the BRIL Board meeting. The BR Board Meeting on 5th November records as an introduction to the presentation of the BRIL document that there had been a meeting with the Secretary of State on 21st October in which the Secretary of State had considered that early action in the disposal of BRIL assets was essential even though this was likely to entail substantial discounts. Property was clearly going to become a major issue and the Secretary of State would be looking for some early progress. Just as BTH Board were brushed aside by BRIL, it seemed that BRIL were being brushed aside by Government.

The Minutes of the BR Board went some way to redress the balance created by the non representative and biased report produced to them by BRIL. This was, of course, the influence of three members of the BR Board who were also members of the BTH Board that had approved the Plan submitted to BRIL. The conclusions of the BR Board were by no means discouraging to us in confirming its commitment to the introduction of private capital into the hotel company "at the earliest possible time" and noting that there were no differences in view on the policy which was fully supported by the BTH Board. They noted the view of BRIL that the delay of cash realisation inherent in the BTH Plan would affect their own short term cash flow but they emphasised the need to keep faith with the Unions on the undertaking about reinvestment and the need to maintain morale in an ongoing business. The BR Board were clearly distressed by phrases like outright sale and disposal and reiterated the fact that every endeavour should be made to maintain an interest by the Board in the ongoing businesses and that the intent should be "to devise projects similar to the GHP and Derby/Sheffield concept". They directed that every effort must be made to reach a reasonable measure of agreement between BRIL and BTH before final proposals were submitted to them for their authority.

What a dilemma. BRIL'S attached advisers endeavoured to make some peace by producing a supplementary paper to their document to BR which did no more than deal with technical matters concerning the rates of tax, PE ratios, discounts on valuations and redundancy payments. There was no way in which immediate disposal could be justified against a carefully planned privatisation following a flotation route in about 2/3 years time when the full benefits of what had already been achieved managerially would bear fruit. To dispose of the business quickly merely meant all the advantages we had worked so hard to achieve would go to a new owner at a price based on the best that could be obtained in the bad times. The only gamble that BRIL had to take was that we could continue to achieve what had been achieved over the past two years. The BTH Board and management team believed that its recent track record entitled it to the support of BRIL, relying on their success in any Political argument. It was clear by the end of November that we were not going to be able to reconcile the views of the BTH management and the young consultants seconded to BRIL. I had to record to my Chairman that the BRIL paper to the BR Board did not accurately or fairly represent the BTH arguments and that in my view we were entitled to expect our arguments to be presented in any paper to the BR Board even if they were rejected by BRIL. I knew perfectly well that BRIL could not produce an argument to beat us, that had any better commercial judgement.

We had spent literally hours in Executive and Non Executive Directors' time preparing a very responsible Plan for the Company and it was totally defeated in the end by the meek acceptance by BRIL that the most important aspect of its work was to achieve things "within the life of this parliament". Overtly, or otherwise, they were now under the political direction we had all feared when they were set up and that what had been seen as a "considerable tactical victory for Sir Peter Parker" had now become little better than a fifth column. Perhaps it was a great pity that Mike Bosworth was such a decent man, liked and respected by us all.

CHAPTER FOURTEEN – THE UNIONS STIRRED

The Company had a very satisfactory history in its relationship with its employees. A closed shop was effectively in operation though technically this was defined as a union shop. Basically, the difference is that in a closed shop an employee is normally a card carrying member before he is taken on but with a union shop he is required to join the union within a specified time of being engaged. Over many years there had been arguments conducted by BR for its entire labour force on the merits of a union shop or not and the conclusion had been arrived at some years earlier that had led to a union shop. In devising and carrying out many very radical changes, both as an Accountant and as a manager in British Rail and the National Freight Corporation over a period of approaching 20 years, I had built up a real respect for the NUR in particular and only marginally less high regard for the Transport Salaried Staff Association. I had, over those years, been able to compare them with the Transport and General Workers Union and learned the relative values of a union concentrating its efforts on a single industry and a union that was concerned with many industries and employers.

Whilst in my career with British Rail and the National Freight Corporation I had guided and been guided by the employees' representatives through many changes, I could see that the introduction of private sector finance, particularly if it were seen to eliminate BR control, would be opening a door through which few of the people in responsible positions in the trade unions had ever passed. The union employed a skilled research team to analyse the problems with which it would be confronted and therefore on which it was desirable for it to form a view. The union officials were always extremely capable of arguing, agreeing and subsequently implementing decisions for change that applied to established practices.

I was confident in my own track record in industrial relations and confident that I had never failed to deliver the management commitment in any agreement, but above all, I had the greatest respect for the men who were leading the union as individuals since never had they failed to deliver what they had agreed.

Toward the end of 1980, the NUR research team had been put to work to provide background briefing notes on British Rail subsidiary businesses and to draw conclusions regarding the organisational changes that were being promulgated by Politicians. The conclusions by that research group were incredibly accurate. At the time of reading them, no-one in the management believed that they were anything but a slightly cynical over statement of possible situations. They were so accurate that it is worth recording much of the detail of what was said by the NUR research group in January 1981.

It was concluded that the subsidiaries, with the exception of the Property Board, were in a poor financial condition and, as a consequence, were placing a strain on the railways' hard pressed finances. In those circumstances it was therefore not surprising that the Board would favour a solution that could loosen the financial strait jacket of looking to private sources of capital.

"Those who work in the subsidiaries had watched jealously as their private sector counterparts – with more ready cash flow- have grabbed the opportunities they were forced to miss for many years."

As investment needs build up the likelihood of Government ever sanctioning the finance required was seen as becoming more and more remote.

The Board had established Sealink as a wholly owned subsidiary company in 1978. This had not altogether left the trade unions happy because, they argued, it was possibly the first stage of a hiving off. To which the Board had replied that if the political will existed to take that course there was little they would be able to do about it. But that was not BR's purpose. The philosophy was to show that if more money could be made available to the subsidiary companies then they could flourish in competition with any of their private sector counterparts.

The unions were critical that the Board's ideas had backfired. An expression that I believe is a little too strong - the ideas had just not fired at all. Once again it had been established that unless the rules were changed by the Treasury, any finance in a subsidiary company over which the Board had control would still be counted as public sector borrowing. With all the benefit of hindsight, the subsequent errors in privatisation were made by not getting those rules sorted out. The matter was not sorted out and the Government made regulations and the inflexibility of the Treasury thinking subsequently wrought havoc when it came to trying to make commercially based business decisions.

Having decided to do something about the subsidiaries, the Government then began to interfere with how the Board should organise the control of its subsidiaries and took the line that a holding company should be set up, wholly in the hands of the Minister so that he could then proceed to transfer the assets of the subsidiaries to the private sector at his will. The Government were deflected from that approach when they discovered that it would put them at severe loggerheads with the British Railways Board. There was a risk that the Board could take the extreme solution and resign en masse. A course not to be commended since they would simply have been replaced by more amenable members and it would have been no more than a political hiccup, forgotten in a month. It must be remembered that resignation of public sector Boards does not cause all that embarrassment. One can recall when the National Enterprise Board, resigned, the Government simply found a new set of people who presumably did not find their policies too troublesome. As often is the case when politicians are inconvenienced by having to face facts, it slowly began to dawn on them and their servants that the BR subsidiaries were not exactly the most profitable, desirable businesses for which buyers would beat a path to their door. The reason for that, of course, had been totally non-commercial financial policies pursued by successive Government over many years. That realisation helped to produce the slightly more flexible solution of setting up a holding company that was wholly owned by the Board. However, it was a solution by which the Government could retain the strongest control over privatisation by using its overall control of the Board as both a carrot and a stick. In some similar circumstances the arrangements might simply be called blackmail.

The Government's change of attitude was seen as a combination of political and practical difficulties. There was the conflict with the Board, the difficulties if any MP's business interests were to lead them to being in any acquisition, the immense problem of justifying the selling prices that could be obtained against the dreams of unreality.

The Transport Bill of December 1980 empowered the British Railways Board, with the consent of the Minister, to dispose of any part of the whole of any subsidiary business. But the Bill also proposed to give power to the Minister to give directions to BRB. This left the Government's tactics perfectly obvious – they would use their control over the external financial limit to regulate the speed of denationalisation and, if the BR Board did not progress along the path of privatisation with sufficient pace, the Government would direct the Board to generate finance through asset sales and reduce the EFL by the funds the holding company would be targeted to generate. All good stuff provided you don't believe when trying to run the business, that your shareholders are actually on your side and that the commercial success is vaguely relevant.

The NUR research group concluded that the Government were not intending that the sale of assets should generate any additional money for railways whatsoever; that whilst the Board had succeeded in preventing the Government going right down the hiving off road because they would retain some control over the programme of privatisation, an unsatisfactory compromise had been reached.

"The Government maintains control of the speed at which private capital is introduced into the subsidiaries and this will lead to restrictions on the methods the Board can use to introduce capital. It also appears that the introduction of private capital into the subsidiaries will be of no direct benefit to the railways".

The Board were seen to have blunted their weapons in their fight to get Government to provide more finance for the railways by this move.

The research group had made an excellent exposition of the subject.

As was so often remarked, particularly by Sir Peter Parker, I had got a very big business to run while everyone was playing around with implementation of a political ideology in which every step was another obstacle to management.

A golden rule in any change is to keep the people who are concerned with that change well informed and as soon as possible. In carrying out this practice we did have one very serious problem. Whilst it was always possible to have informal discussion with the senior people in the National Union of Railwaymen and conduct that discussion as much as anything on the basis of exchanging views on how best to achieve a particular objective, it was not possible to have similar discussions with the Transport Salaried Staff Association whose General Secretary was obliged to reveal all discussions immediately to his Executive and his members through his journal. The result was a better industrial relation practice with the NUR where it was possible to debate options in any particular field off the record and try to find those which were mutually acceptable. If then, in the negotiations with other investors, it was possible to include these options then clearly a smooth path was being laid for the subsequent change. If, on the other hand, every time one wanted to consider options for the way to implement something, the next edition of the union's newspaper contained them as headlines, there was no way in which one could move along any path other than that of presenting them with a fait accompli. This weakened considerably the TSSA's own position in contributing to the thoughts about change.

The information discussions took the union to the point of deciding how best to introduce the topics to their sometimes difficult and even militant Executive and, they came round to the view that I should be invited to speak to the full NUR Executive Committee and their principal officers. This was no easy task and both the President and General Secretary knew that to be a success the whole thing had to be very carefully managed otherwise Daniel in Lion's Den was going to be a bedtime story compared with what would happen to me. We worked carefully together on the outline of the paper that I was to present. We identified the no go areas and on 4th March I presented myself to the Executive Committee for rather more than two hours.

As was to be anticipated, it was no easy ride. I was given a very good hearing and then a very sound beating by some of the more belligerent and politically motivated members. But, at the end of it all, we had a very high mutual respect for each other's point of view and, above all, a conviction that we were actually all working for the benefit of the employees of BTH since, if BTH did not succeed as a business then there was no future for the employment anyway. The EC were left with no misunderstanding that the laundries were going to close; that the BTH Board believed it to be in the interests of the Company to introduce private sector capital; that we should continue to have control over money raised by any sale of assets; and that political decisions should not override good business considerations.

Much of the argument that came back was pressing me to prove to their satisfaction that I could live with my commitment to the employees, that whatever happened they would enter a new employer's organisation on exactly the same conditions and terms that they had with BTH including provision of travel, pension rights and the like. I was convinced that I could do this but, I also pointed out that was the end of my responsibility. We could not commit any new owners, and I emphasised that trade unions would have to learn to deal with a new employer who might not be large corporation of the style of British Rail but might actually be a single hotel owner whose ancestors had not necessarily lived in this country. I was not too sure that they could live in that world. They appreciated the problem and my only disappointment at that meeting was that one person mentioned slightly in excitement that if they didn't like something, they "would stop the railway". I thought that was foolish but perhaps I had better assessment than the EC member of the future fights with trade unions for which some members of Government were preparing.

The transfer of staff to be employees of Gleneagles Hotels plc was successfully carried out and great care was taken to ensure that the trade unions met the potential new owners well in advance so that any problems or attitudes could be properly sorted out. This was important to ensure that the new owners saw the union representatives in their true colours as perfectly reasonable people with all the normal anxieties that loss of livelihood could bring. The transfer was accompanied by an excellent front page article in the NUR news of July 1981 concluding that

"the Union has entered into the arrangements with some reluctance but faced with the possible closure of the North British Hotel under the previous arrangements and accepting the present economic recession it was felt there was no acceptable alternative which would safe-guard the ongoing employment of its members".

That was the end of an important beginning which then moved into asking questions about what was to happen to the proceeds and the action that BR proposed to take to follow the Secretary of State's statement in Parliament that he hoped British Rail would invest in further hotel activity.

On 2nd June 1981, there was a meeting between Sir Peter Parker and Sidney Weighell at which Mr. Weighell reiterated the difficulty he had had in persuading his Executive Committee to accept the idea of privatisation and that he would be in grave difficulty if the £6 million received as part of the deal that set up Gleneagles Hotels PLC were not deployed for British Rail Investments Limited or BTH purposes. He particularly emphasised that he did not wish to see it lost in BR general funds. The Chairman of British Rail agreed to send Mr. Weighell a letter that he hopes would be helpful to him in handling his problem. The letter was duly sent on 3rd June and confirmed that the Board had no reason to assume that the proceeds accruing to BR from the Gleneagles transaction would not be available for general BR purposes in the same way that proceeds from property sales had been made available.

"indeed we would take a dim view of any proposal which did other than enable the Board to benefit from the total proceeds of any sales of assets."

A perfectly acceptable statement for anyone. Indeed, I recall personally at one of my annual presentations to the full British Railways Board, over the lunch that followed, Lord Caldicott saying that I must understand that, if in the interests of the Board finances as a whole, it was necessary to sell British Transport Hotels, it was the benefit of the whole which was more significant. I fully accepted that position as being the only correct position in any conglomerate, providing we were not selling the family silver to pay the butcher's bill. With a Treasury whose accountancy ends with a cash account closed at each fiscal year end, and a Government concerned with transactions within the life " of this Parliament", I could only hope that BR could actually control their finances on the lines of Lord Caldecott's statement.

With that assurance, the matter rested for a short time when on 8th October, the General Secretary of the NUR reminded the Chairman of his letter, saying that

"it would be helpful to my Union if you could assure me that the bulk of these proceeds could be used for BTH development" and going on to say that if that assurance could be given he would be able to finalise the proposals that were before them for Derby and Sheffield but, at the same time, being disturbed by a statement that had been made at a BR Council Meeting that indicated that BRIL had already made the decisions concerning Derby/Sheffield and that the laundries were also to be disposed of which was quite contrary to the way we had been successfully working in conducting our own industrial relations in the Company. For the first time, the NUR were now seeing another set of people emerging in the decision taking process with whom they had no relationships whatsoever and who apparently were making decisions about business in which the NUR were an accredited trade union.

It is fairly clear that the NUR had wind of the difficulties that Sir Alexander Glen and myself had been having in the submission of our Plan to British Rail Investments. I was authorised to give the NUR a copy of the Plan which, at that stage, I would have certainly not done without the authority of the Chairman of British Rail because it would place the BR Board in an embarrassing position. The Plan proposed by the BTH Board would have been perfectly acceptable to the trade unions and we would have not the slightest difficulty in getting their full support for it since it demonstrated the re-investment of a certain amount of money that was being obtained from privatisation; the expansion of the business and its development to make it an acceptable proposition for flotation in 1984. But there was that expression that the hotel company was to be disposed of during the life of the present parliament. On the other hand, there was the policy statement from British Railways Board of intended continued financial interest in any privatised unit; there was the Chairman's letter of June indicating the use of proceeds from any privatisation for the benefit of BR and, above all, there was a BTH Plan that required no financial support from BR and therefore no drain on financing limits. By 19th November, having had the opportunity to study the Plan, the General Secretary of the NUR wrote to me, indicating that they would not be able to proceed any further with implementing the Plan or in particular the proposals for Derby and Sheffield or the laundries "until the prerequisite assurances are made in respect of the use of the capital of the schemes".

There was no difficulty in being able to demonstrate that the capital expenditure programme for BTH and Sealink far outweighed the proceeds from realisation and a letter was duly sent in January 1982. This simply related the proceeds from privatisation to the capital expenditure proposed in the Plan. A Plan that had by now been shelved, if not actually rejected by BRIL. It took no account whatsoever of the normal spending of the provision for depreciation. There was nothing untrue in the reply but had the Union had good accountancy advice they would have torn the response to shreds for what it failed to say. Any business should be spending its depreciation provision but when the total capital programme is only of that level and, in addition, there is £6 million of asset realisation, you are simply being misled if you accept that cash realised from asset sales had been used in the capital programme.

The subject was slowly talked out and other matters began to be demanding the attention of the EC, not the least of which was the enormous problem of rostering.

Had the unions been able to play their cards with good professional backing in the field of accountancy, they could have really taken BR to the cleaners, but they were in a field in which they had insufficient experience and they could but whimper. A great deal was lost by the failure of the unions to fight the point of reinvestment. They could have won easily but they became distracted by arguments and fights which aroused much more in the short term the more militant members of their Executive. They were driven into backing a loser in form of believing it mattered if they stopped the Railway whereas they failed to back the winner which was to fight Politicians and BR Board to deliver their statements of intent.

CHAPTER FIFTEEN –MANAGEMENT SUCCESSES OF 1981

The line management seized its opportunity to use the authority delegated to it. Quietly, they had got on with the important problem of reducing the number of staff employed and an achievement of 16% reduction was the best we had achieved and far outweighed any other performance in British Rail.

The decision of BR that we were to segregate the Travellers-Fare part of our business and transfer it back into railway line management was an unwelcome managerial burden without which we could well have done. But it was all achieved by the appointed date of 1st January 1982.

To achieve a reduction of 16% in staff demanded very close working with all the levels of the trade unions. But, in addition to achieving reduction, considerable progress was made in the introduction of flexible working hour arrangements. In 1981 staff costs were actually less than in 1980 in spite of a high inflation rate.

We had designed a new hotel in the grounds of the Royal Station Hotel, York, designed specifically to meet the needs of tourist business related to travel by bus. Friars Garden was a splendid achievement and gave a lot of encouragement to the staff to see the company expanding its activity and particularly moving away in that expansion from the classic image of BTH.

We had been studying our needs at Turnberry for some time and concluded that there was a need to introduce some better facilities for the holiday market who needed more than golf. To do this, we built a new sports and leisure complex designed to work closely with the conference facilities that had already been created. So far as we were concerned, Turnberry was thus complete and, in due course, we could begin to return attention to the golf and probably think in terms of tracks to enable golf buggies to be introduced and possibly, therefore, appeal to the older golfer from the more affluent end of the American golfing market. Subject to keeping up with regular maintenance and decoration programmes, we saw Turnberry as well established for some time and it was now up to the Manager to perform to his obvious potential.

The Manor House at Moretonhampstead was to be next on our list for getting right and here we saw three principal needs. There was the need for a conference facility as opposed to the meeting room with the green baize table, the development of the stable block as time share or self catering facilities and the need for a swimming pool. The area finally decided upon for conference facilities, as a result of some ingenious thinking by the Manager, was clearly going to lead us into some problems with planners, since it involved splitting the magnificent cathedral lounge horizontally. It was with some trepidation that we argued our way through the Planning Authority and, with a certain amount of apprehension that we watched the early stages of the reconstruction. Designers, architects and the various professions did a magnificent job, leaving practically no sign that what is there was not original. Early discussions were taking place concerning the development of the stable block in such a way to enable us to have sufficient money to build a swimming pool. We saw the conclusion but at the end of 1981 were not taking account of those who were trying to stop us.

The planning of the Welcombe Hotel at Stratford was completed. Here was one of the few occasions where the new management team felt that there had not been a well thought out scheme introduced by its predecessors. Fundamentally, all that

119

had happened was that a golf course had been built without any thought being given to the effect it would have on the Hotel and without any proper provision for the people who were going to use the golf course. The Welcombe is a country house type of hotel and therefore needed extremely careful thought when introducing a modern conference facility and bar arrangements. It was vital to encourage visitors to come to the hotel purely for the purpose of using the bar and restaurant. An excellent development was completed just in time for the new owners to reap all the benefit.

The Tregenna Castle Hotel had a small nine-hole golf course and having looked very carefully at adjoining land that was owned by the Company, it was seen as possible to produce an 18 hole golf course, albeit one that was designed more for the holiday golfer than for serious player. This was a wonderful achievement in that the whole job was completed almost entirely by the ground staff of the hotel which of itself gave them a tremendous lift.

We pursued our policy of getting rid of the classic hotel dining room and in the City Gates at the Great Eastern Hotel, Liverpool Street and the Betjamen Restaurant at Charing Cross, produced partially self-service restaurants second to none and these became immediate successes.

At Hull and Liverpool, the more popular type of facilities were introduced to replace the formal dining room.

New bars were built in Inverness and Charing Cross where, in addition to the Jubilee and Pullman Bars being opened, the great excitement of taking over the Griffin Public House was achieved. This was a pub that had for many years been leased and, on expiry of the lease, we succeeded in getting control.

For years we had concealed the fact that we sold drink in the Great Northern Hotel at King's Cross and the opening of Potters Bar in a position where it could be well seen from the station forecourt and had a very easy access near the hotel door, had a significant effect of the revenue of that hotel. Probably the most exciting bar project of the year was the conversion of old staff quarters at the Lochalsh Hotel into the Ferry Boat Inn. Again, some good vision by the Executive Director and the Hotel

Manager enabled this small site with its magnificent views to the Isle of Skye to be developed into a very attractive little pub.

In our last year of control of Travellers-Fare, we invested in building the Tropics Bar in Glasgow. This was an enterprising venture which again met the objective of taking Travellers-Fare away from its image of catering only where trains could be seen. This is an interesting site under Glasgow's 'umbrella' with outside street entrance. It was designed with a theme that would attract young people and its merchandise was similarly planned. Another major development in Travellers-Fare was the theme of jazz in the new facilities at Liverpool Street Station.

In America we enjoyed great success, having moved from Queens into Manhattan and shaken off the image in the company that we were only something to do with railways. The business developed its own tours and many different packages. Tactically we only made a song and dance about these achievements once they were a fait accompli. This was because of the BR tie where their company in the States was a personal power base. Anything set up that did not prompt rail as the mode of transport in the UK was not encouraged. We had the base of a tour operator and were not to be constrained to one form of transport.

1981 was an absolutely fascinating year in which to manage such a large organisation. People were responding to the initiatives that the BTH Board had set them. The first faltering steps in the path of privatisation had been successfully carried out and at the same time, all the disasters that were to follow were being identified. The ultimate inevitable victory of the political ideology and the establishment was apparent yet all of this had to be kept from those who were working so hard to make the business a commercial success and it was being so aware of this that, in January 1982, when I did a short review of the achievement of 1981 for the staff I concluded,

"There will be great change in 1982 from which stability will emerge. The exact form of that stability cannot be predicted yet. Strength will come from success".

It is interesting to look back and see that within their new environment, the successful Manager of 1981 survived with their new owners, even though, as the hotels were traded as properties, little stability was achieved.

CHAPTER SIXTEEN – THE BUY OUT INITIATIVE

It was towards the end of 1981 that, when the BTH Board's business proposals to BRIL ceased to be talked about, we accepted that the Company, in its present form, had very limited life. The first time the possibility of a fight from the employees of the business was suggested was when I was invited to take lunch with the BRIL Board. During the meal, I suggested that, in their thinking for any disposal, they would want to presume that a management buy out would be one of their options. I sensed that such a proposal was received initially with shock. As we talked through the possibility, the members of the BRIL Board who were present saw merit in the idea. So much so, that a hotel sub committee of British Rail Investments Limited was formed to go into some of the detail. We had several informal meetings into the night and we agreed that, together with my colleagues John Tee and Derek Plant, I would put forward an outline proposal for discussion.

This was done by mid February 1982 and proposed that a new company would be created to purchase a selection of the hotels, to take others on by way of management contracts and to assist BRIL for the time it took to dispose of the remainder. It indicated the desire to create the opportunity for full staff participation in equity. There were two major problems arising.

The first concerned the actual titles of the property. Some presented no problem since they were totally removed from any other railway property, but others (and good examples were Charing Cross, the Grosvenor Victoria, Queens Leeds and the Royal Station Hull) were integral parts of railway stations. Decisions had to be taken which we accepted might result in certain properties not actually being freeholds. Having gone through these agonies, particularly with the North British Hotel Edinburgh a year or so before, we recognised that the problems were troublesome but certainly not insurmountable, provided one behaved with determination and goodwill, using a reasonable amount of commonsense.

The second, somewhat less clear, problem concerned the inevitable question that somebody somewhere and sometime was going to ask about what the hotels were worth. Work, which seemed to be run by Morgan Grenfell, had been set in hand some little time earlier that had set Christie & Co. and Druce & Co. jointly to establish a valuation. Why on earth we needed two firms, I will never understand. Clearly, we for our part would be more concerned with a valuation based on what we believed the hotels could earn since it was our intention to go into the business on the basis of being hoteliers and not being property speculators. We realised, of course, that strong competition in the event of any sale would come from the latter. We also felt it rather important that these superb British establishments should continue to be British owned and operated. We knew that, in the event of any sale, ongoing British ownership was pretty unlikely.

The meetings of the hotel sub committee were chaired by Mike Bosworth and, whilst we debated different views about the many aspects of how the business could be constructed, financed and controlled, there was never any doubt in our minds that we were all working for a similar end.

Towards the end of February, we had considered our entire proposal together and formed the view as to how a formal proposal should be constructed. This was a most sensible and balanced way to approach the task. Whilst clearly the day must arise when we had to move into a slightly arm's length negotiating position, it was of paramount importance at this stage that the management team working to construct a buy out proposal should approach as many problems as possible in the best way to help BRIL through their dealings with their masters, and their master's advisers.

Work began in earnest and a draft was submitted on 10th March 1982. Again, it must be recalled that, at that time, there had been no indication given as to the valuation that the professional valuers would put on the hotels or on any qualification they might add to their valuation, when any constraints that BR may wish to impose were known.

In submitting our proposal, we had been told that BR wished to impose, because of its long term international requirements, the following encumbrances on our properties:

(a)   a resumption over the area of the hotel in Leeds that housed the boilers;

(b)   to withdraw its responsibility for the provision of heating to the Great Western Hotel in five years' time;

(c)   a resumption over the area of the Grosvenor Victoria occupied by the kitchen in 12 years' time;

(d)   a resumption over the main banqueting area in the Grosvenor Victoria in 12 years' time;

(e)   to exclude all the retail shops that are part of the Grosvenor;

(f)   to include the Charing Cross only on a 20 year lease on the main building;

(g)   to offer a lease on the Great Northern Hotel of only five years.

They were not silly encumbrances of the result of anyone trying to be difficult. There was perfectly good operational argument from BR in respect of each item. Our reaction to them was constructive and helpful. We suggested, in the case of the Great Western Royal, because we saw even greater property integration that it would be much better to put the hotel on the same basis as the Charing Cross, that is a 20 year lease. We were not happy with a proposal for a five year lease on the Great Northern because, whilst we appreciated that there would be property development in that area, in a hotel business five years is insufficient time to justify any serious investment. Whilst we understood the problems operationally so far as BR were concerned with the Grosvenor being such an integral part of Victoria Station, we did feel that we should try to remove their rights to take over this kitchen and the banqueting area in only 12 years for the fairly obvious reason that a hotel without a kitchen does have one or two operational problems. We had also spent rather a lot of money in the basement of the Grosvenor making good working conditions for staff and thus already eliminated a major area for future kitchen development or replacement.

Our submission of 10th March was still essentially a discussion document constructed together with the Officers of British Rail Investments Limited. On 12th March, the valuers produced their valuations which indicated a view that the London Hotels might be worth £28.5 million, those in the provinces worth £16.6 million and those in Scotland worth £7.9 million. A total of £53 million.

As was expected, the figures had to be read in conjunction with many conditions and reservations. The following were the major conditions:-

1.   Where a formal lease did not exist, a new 125 year lease would be granted at a nominal ground rent fixed for the entire term.

2.   Where the dividing off of services provided to the hotel from other railway premises had to be undertaken that the cost of those changes would be provided by the vendor.

3.   The valuation excluded any ongoing expenditure that a purchaser might have to incur in respect of compensation to existing staff, costs of redundancy and the termination of fringe benefits such as free travel allowances, etc.

4.   A recommendation that a decision to sell off any individual hotel should not be taken until the question of a group disposal had been thoroughly investigated.

These were very important conditions. As will be seen, this valuation became the cornerstone of argument until the middle of November 1982. It was predictable that the figure of £53 million became fixed in minds without paying any attention to the very important qualifications placed on their figures by the valuers. This was grossly unfair to the valuers and, in due course, became very unfair to us. The Christie/Druce team were at pains to remind the BRIL Board on 1st March 1983 when the results of the tender were being considered and everyone was trying to prove that their advice had really been good, that their valuation had been reduced by £3 million because the purchaser was required to pay costs of segregating property and to take over the cost of staff travel facilities. This is a very important point to keep in mind as the next stages of this area unfold. Bureaucrats, their advisers and Politicians became obsessed with judging everything against a valuation built on shifting sand.

It was not important to move quickly towards a formal submission by making changes to the draft that were found mutually desirable and any further changes that we felt desirable. We thus began to move to an arm's length relationship. Our own advisers Kleinwort Benson, now began to play a very significant role and it was with their support that on 14th June we made a formal submission seeking agreement in priniciple by 9th July, with a completion objective of 31st October 1981. This was to meet a timetable laid down by BRIL and made on the basis of property titles being as stated by the valuers in their qualifications in their letter of 12th March.

The proviso in the valuation assuming that there would be a good freehold, or leasehold title for 125 years, caused a great deal of problem to BR. Obviously, it was imperative that we knew the precise conditions on which property would pass before we submitted our proposal but this could not be achieved. After much toing and froing, practically none of which was the making of BTH, we were given the basis upon which we were to base our proposal on 17th June with the proviso that we would submit it not later than 25th June, after which we would be informed as quickly as possible if our offer was acceptable and then given two weeks to confirm our offer after discussions with our merchant bank advisers.

To ensure that we were taken seriously, Kleinwort Benson wrote on our behalf to the Board on 14th June

"the position now is that upon receipt of your confirmation that you would, in principle be prepared to accept an offer on the lines discussed, we would proceed to formulate a proposal which would then be subject only to contract and to a very limited number of conditions such as a satisfactory accountant's report and confirmation of title and taxation clearances or indemnities."

In the same letter they felt that it was "relevant here to outline the basis on which we have been developing our preliminary conclusion that the group scheme was practicable." They also pointed out that those interested in providing the funds would be concerned with assets only to the extent that they provide a cushion and a base for borrowing

"the key to successful financing will lie in the projected profitability of the business and the faith placed by potential investors in the ability of the management to achieve its target".

It was on this basis rather than on estimated asset values that we arrived at our outline proposals. We were approaching the whole project from the basis of an ongoing business and certainly not as property speculators.

Since the end of 1981, there had constantly been the buzz that the only way to deal with the disposal of BTH was by a tender in which everyone should have an equal chance to bid. We had argued consistently that, in our opinion, if the BR Board accepted an instruction to sell by a tender procedure, then it was unlikely that we would be able to participate. Kleinwort Benson, in their letter of 14th June, took the opportunity to state this position

"to say at the outset that so far as we are aware a contest of the nature envisaged would be without precedent at least in recent years in the City. This does not mean of course that new ground cannot be broken but it does add to the uncertainty in seeking to make a specific competitive proposal".

This letter was acknowledged by the Board on 18th June in a letter that noted that Kleinwort Benson did not consider that it would be possible for the management buy out group to put in a bid as part of the open tender offer "we are proposing" and understood

"that if we are to seek offers via the tender procedure for individual hotels, groups of hotels, or the total package then it would clearly be difficult to process the management buy out on such a basis.

"we therefore have to consider whether to accept an offer from the group prior to the tender offer or realise that the group cannot proceed beyond the current stage".

We had made an offer fully supported by a leading Merchant Bank, and in its reply, BRIL acknowledged that we could not proceed if they elected to sell by tender.

The proposal was that a new company would be formed to purchase as freehold or as 125 years leasehold, sixteen of the hotels and take short leases on the Charing Cross and the Great Northern for 20 years and 10 years respectively. An opportunity was sought to take a management contract on the Great Eastern Hotel and the Central Hotel Glasgow. The proposal thus covered all hotels in the group with the exception of Liverpool, Aberdeen and the North British, Glasgow. All the terms and conditions of employment of staff were accepted together with all constraints BR placed on the properties.

The price offered was £29 million plus stock at valuation to be met by £19 million on completion and the balance in four equal instalments at the end of years 2 to 5. We believed that the valuation of these properties placed by Christies/Druce to be £35/£36 million. We did not know of the fact to be disclosed on 1st March 1983 that, when the conditions and encumbrances became known, the valuers reduced that valuation by £3 million. We pointed out that, if the Board were willing to deal with us directly, they would avoid the commission to be paid to their selling agents, avoid the fees to their financial advisers and minimise legal and accountancy fees, points not necessarily attractive to those advisers! The Board would avoid a delay of five months that it would take to implement an alternative and not only earn interest on the realisation but avoid any trading losses during that period. In our view, if full values were bid in a tender for these properties, the net realisation would not exceed £30 million when all costs and fees were taken into account. Had we known, as presumably BRIL did, that the properties had been revalued £3 million lower than our information, then our opinion of £30 million would have been reduced to £28 million.

Whilst our price offered was £29 million, £10 million was to be paid in instalments over years 2 to 5. If this sum were discounted at 15% per annum, its present value would be in the order of £7.5 million. Thus the net present value of our offer was £26.5 million. Thus against our knowledge as to the valuation, there was a shortfall of £3.5 million. The facts said to be available to BRIL showed the gap as only £1.5 million.

It was open to BR to decide if they wished to become minority shareholders in the new company. So far as we were concerned, not only were they most welcome, they would be positively encouraged. We had no embarrassment, ill feeling, or other concern about an ongoing interest of our railway colleagues, particularly if we could have that interest of them as people freed from political direction as to their thinking.

Our proposal had the advantages that it was backed by a leading merchant bank and it gave an opportunity for staff to have equity participation. We saw the proposal as a responsible reaction to Government policy and one which could be implemented quicker than any alternative and dealt with the privatisation of hotels in one arrangement.

So far as BR was concerned, it ensured ongoing employment for 86% of the staff. Over the weeks, we had worked closely with the General Secretaries of the two trade unions involved and were able to indicate that in the event of acceptance, the proposals would have their unqualified support. Thus, our proposal had the important value that, at a time when IR problems were beginning to amount in BR, this was a development which would have no industrial relation repercussions. Politically it had the advantage of involving the Trade Unions in a piece of privatisation to which in principle they were completely opposed

We were naturally elated when a meeting of the BR Board Executive on 8th July supported the buy out. Mr. Bosworth presented the document to the Executive who expressed the view of the value of a smooth transaction which this method of sale offered as being most important. BR Board Executive felt that if maximum cash realisation was the sole aim then the tender option must be endorsed but, they acknowledged that the trading position could suffer while tenders were being considered and tender offers could be low because of the general state of the hotels. Certainty of sale and smooth transition were cogent factors and it was seen as pertinent that an independent merchant bank firmly supported the management buy out and hence the management behind the proposal. There was therefore seen to be a good case to support this

"self generated proposal before further pressure was applied by Government to raise cash by the release of assets".

The Executives supported the management buy out proposal subject to the level of discount achieving a gap between the offer and the valuation within the range £3 million to £5 million. Obviously this was effectively a total acceptance since there was no problem whatsoever in bridging a gap of the magnitude indicated.

Immediately we met with Kleinwort Benson, changed the terms of payment of our offer, pointed out a couple of changes BRIL would want to make on the valuation where certain things had not been taken into account and thus achieved the closing of the gap by a further £2 million, thus making an offer greater than the valuation known to BRIL. At a Board Executive on 22nd July, Mr. Bosworth was able to report that all members of the Board had been consulted on the issue of the buy out and that a letter had been sent to the Department of Transport giving details of the proposals. Whilst it was noted that there was no certainty that the proposal would be supported by the Department, the Chairman indicated that he would endeavour to raise the matter with the Secretary of State at an informal meeting on 23rd July. The same meeting noted that the proposed buy out could not be made as a bid through the tender procedure. Mr.Bosworth was able to report that BRIL felt that a discount of 5% on the valuation was a reasonable reflection of the value of the elimination of such uncertainties which the tender option would incur. This discount did not include any benefits that could be derived from the possible removal of industrial relations uncertainties which could only be assessed by the Board. It was reported that a total discount of £4.5 million therefore could be justified.

A very important point of procedure arose at that meeting where, on the one hand, it is reported that there is no certainty that the proposal will be supported by the Department, but also that the Chairman will endeavour to raise the matter with the

Secretary of State. This clearly identifies the two different problems with which the Chairman of BR always had to wrestle. On the one hand there was the political problem, on the other hand, there was the bureaucratic problem; both of which of course had to be right in the end and preferably be protected, so that if anything should go wrong, they could shift entire responsibility to the Chairman of British Rail.

This was, of course, no different from the situation that had arisen with Gleneagles where the Secretary of State slipped out of all responsibility for the actual sale of the assets by saying that he only gave approval for BR to acquire shares in a new company – it was a matter for the Chairman of BR to justify the price at which he sold off his assets. Here, taking note of what happened then, we had put a case together by which, provided BR did not take equity in the new company, they had no need ever to seek the approval of the Secretary of State because his predecessor had established the principle that it was the responsibility of the Chairman of BR to decide the price at which he sold his assets. He only needed Secretary of State approval to take equity in a new company. No Chairman of a public sector business in his right mind would dispose of £30 million of his assets without keeping his minister informed. This is no more than a matter of common courtesy.

Questions that began to come back from British Rail Investments Limited were obviously influenced by civil servants' questions addressed to BRIL. Two things appeared to be causing some concern in their anxiety to reject the proposal. First there was the problem of employee participation. Politically, it was clearly going to be dangerous to reject something which had fairly high employee participation in the equity. The main problem was said to be

"how many shares will be taken up by staff and management at the commencement of the new company".

There was no-one more desperate than I to be able to put to the staff a firm proposition and invite their participation. But for some reason, no-one would understand that we could not begin to canvass commitment of the staff until Kleinwort Benson had been given the authority to approach all potential investors. I explained, that before employees could give any sensible indication of their likely interest, they would want to know more about what they were being asked to subscribe for and the likely return on their investment. It was my view that it would be counter productive because of the uncertainty involved, to make any vague approaches to individuals at the hotels until we had a firm acceptance of the offer that we had made. We were confident of a very high response from individuals. I could also imagine the likelihood of approaching 2,400 individuals and still keeping the matter out of the press because, so far as I was concerned and so far as our advisers were concerned, the whole business was a confidential matter between ourselves and the BR Board. There was no way that I was going to take any steps that resulted in the press finding out what was going on.

There was also nervousness about the possibility of us buying some of the hotels and then selling them at a fairly fat profit within a very short space of time (with the benefit of hindsight this concern is a particularly sick joke!) Since this matter had been considered carefully and proposals made that were acceptable at the time we did the Gleneagles deal, we had no difficulty in saying we would find the same terms acceptable. That is to say if we sold any of the properties within a specified period of time, a proportion of any profit would be paid to the original owners.

It is quite remarkable that no such constraint was to be placed on any of the purchasers under the subsequent tender arrangements and probably not at all surprising that within hours of the sale being completed under tender, some hotels were being traded. The Government and bureaucrats had no need to fear the honesty of our intention to hold an important group of hotels together as a trading concern.

Morgan Grenfell, Christie & Co., and Druce & Co. had formed themselves into a very strong team, setting out the details to be circulated to interested parties in the event of the tender document proceeding. All of their costs and fees could, of course, be avoided by a deal being made with the buy out group.

There were frequent meetings and a number of BTH and Railway people had been placed on the working party to help. There was an interesting meeting on 30th July 1982 chaired by

Morgan Grenfell at which Mr. Bosworth attended and reported that a decision was possible from the Minister about the buy out during the early part of the week commencing 2nd August. If this decision was favourable to the management team, then there would be a pause in the tender process until it was certain that necessary funds could be raised by Kleinwort Benson. If the decision were not immediately favourable, there would still be a hold for six weeks in the timetable for the tender process to allow for any industrial relations repercussions from the decision to follow the tender route. This was a very important meeting because effectively Mike Bosworth put these professional advisers on notice that they might not be required for very much longer.

On Sunday 1st August, the Sunday Telegraph contained the full story which was almost word perfect about the submission and contained the conclusion that

"a management group headed by British Transport Hotels' Managing Director Peter Lamd will be told that despite obtaining British Rail's informal agreement to sell the hotels to them the Minister has decided to put the hotels up for sale by tender."

Where such a leak could possibly had come from remains a mystery but one thing that is absolutely certain is that there was nothing to be gained by the management team engineering such a leak. Up to this stage, we could not have had greater support than we obtained from the Chairman of the Board of British Rail. It must be said that sometimes throughout the three months leading up to our final submission we were not always sure which side BRIL were on but, in fairness to them, they were only doing their job in establishing that their support for our proposals was fully justifiable.

In the week following that disclosure, I was shown the letter written by Sir Peter Parker to the Secretary of State which commended our proposals and we were told that the Secretary of State was urging the Chairman to change his mind on the course that he had taken. On 9th August 1982, I felt it my place to write to Sir Peter Parker to thank him for the support that he had given us by his letter. I reminded him that he and I had discussed in February some ideas and how he had greatly encouraged us. In fact one sensed that he would have loved to have swopped jobs at that time and been a bit of a pirate. I summarised what we had delivered as follows:-

1.   A proposal that met Government policy to get the business out of the public sector.

2.   A protection for BR against asset stripping.

3.   An ability for employees to participate in the ownership of equity.

4.   Flexibility for BR to take or not to take equity interest.

5.   To provide £20 million of cash on completion which together with other realisations from BTH would provide £25 million in the 1982/83 fiscal year.

6.   A proposal that met all the property constraints placed by BR where hotels were connected to stations.

7.   A scheme that would have no industrial relations repercussions.

8.   A proposal that was supported by several groups of people with sound business judgement; Kleinwort Benson; Peat Marwick Mitchell & Co.; the BTH Board; the BR Executive and the BR Board.

I expressed by firm conviction that following this tremendous effort by our team over four months, we had delivered a quality proposal that met all objectives and which could be defended before public accounts committees, select committees and anywhere else because it was both straight and honest. I concluded my letter to Sir Peter Parker, and in hindsight hope it was not considered impertinent, saying,

"I believe the decision is in your hands. I understand pressures are being brought to seek your co-operation to withdraw support. You will see how important it is to all of us in this business of great international standing and tradition that you are able to resist those pressures and hold the decision that you and your colleagues have taken".

Our proposals were referred back by the Secretary of State to BR for three reasons:-

1.   That the level of the offer resulted in a substantial discount compared with the valuation prepared by the independent agents.   This reason was to become a most important point as discussions continued over the next three months because never had there been the slightest indication and never was there to be the slightest indication as to what price or level of discount that would be acceptable.

2.   It is known that a large number of groups within the private sector had expressed interest in the hotels. That proved one of the biggest misjudgements of the century when the time came to open the dozen or so envelopes that responded to the subsequent tender.

3.   That the proposition of risk capital to be taken up by the staff was not substantial. As we had explained time and time again, we were not able to express an opinion about the amount that would be taken up since we hadn't got a deal on which to construct a proposal to the staff. At this stage people were very nervous, of course, about what had happened in Amersham International and in the National Freight Consortium.   In the case of Amersham International there was a large body of public opinion being expressed that the shares had been underpriced and the press were making the most of it.   There were many comments being made about the fact that the Secretary of State had netted only £6 million for the whole assets of NFC. The deal was brilliantly carried out by the NFC management but they created a problem for us, however, by forcing Bureaucrats and Politicians to actually reach a decision on price and stick to it. The dangers in this were enormous and there was no way they were going to take another commercial decision. I recall well speaking to my old colleague, Peter Thompson, at a dinner one night at the RAF Club at the time this problem was at its height. He said to me "the one thing you want to make absolutely certain is to get them to agree the price." Very sound but it was really only summarising our problem.   Never would the politicians or bureaucrats make any positive contribution to the discussions in the sense one expects of the other side in conducting a negotiation. Negotiation with a sponge is the best analogy.

We were able to demonstrate that so far as the staff participating in equity was concerned, we were putting £2 million at the disposal of the staff which represented 6.9% of the total equity and loan capital of £29 million. The NFC deal which was constantly being quoted to us on the basis that the staff subscribed over half the equity. Actually, the participation by the staff that we were planning to achieve was about the same since, in the NFC sale, the staff subscribed for half of the equity, £3.8 million out of an equity and loan capital of £58.5 million. The whole point was quite irrelevant to the business issue at stake.

Great play was made of the fact that the proposal had not been rejected but that it had only been referred back and clearly, in any subsequent discussions, BRIL would be using the help of their merchant bankers, Morgan Grenfell. Obviously, we wished to succeed and we were therefore obliged to begin to construct a new proposal.

Too many people 'hoped' that some satisfactory solution could be found but it was a matter of moral courage, laying one's jobs on the line for a principle, standing up and being counted. More than hope was needed!

CHAPTER SEVENTEEN – THE SECOND PROPOSAL

Some of the relationships were difficult to understand in the period between the rejection of the first submission and the decision to sell by tender. With the benefit of hindsight, they are even more difficult to understand but at the time, one had to try to form clear views on the people who were real friends and supporters, those who wanted to be on the winning side and, regrettably, those who were in it for the fee.

The extremes were clear. One was the political objective and the rejection letter left us in fear that however it might be disguised, the emphasis was going to be a political decision and not a business judgement. The other was the Board of BTH who had an understanding of what had been achieved and could see the Company was now poised to reap the benefits of all the changes that had been made over three years or so and who were anxious for a satisfactory business solution that would take the company into the private sector.

There were a great many people expressing the wish that we, as a buyout group, would succeed and that the Company would be held together but either they lacked power or they were unwilling to die for their principles. During this period, I was convinced, and with hindsight am still convinced, that my own

Company Chairman, Mike Bosworth, who had the difficult task of being Chairman of British Rail Investments Limited and also Deputy Chairman of British Railways Board, was on our side and fought as long and as strongly as he possible could to achieve the BTH Board objective. We had our difficulties with some BRIL Board Members who displayed that dangerous enthusiasm of knowing the solution provided they could use the facts that existed elsewhere. In the end a proposal was made which BRIL supported. It was essential to keep discussions going with the political masters and all their agents. This was an enormous test of patience but, as Mike Bosworth many times told me during those three months, "we could get an answer within 24 hours but it would be no." We were up against the classic Political/Bureaucratic problem of finding a solution that provided belt, braces, pins and left them on the fence with their hands in their pockets.

At the time, and looking back on those times, my greatest confusion was, I believe, caused by not being able to comprehend the position held by Morgan Grenfell. They were advisers to British Rail Board and to British Rail Investments Limited. BTH, whilst they were a subsidiary of those two companies, were having to pursue their submission at arm's length. A perfectly sensible arrangement was being made by which Kleinwort Benson were to be the merchant bankers advising BTH. The greatest difficulty was that Morgan Grenfell also appeared to be advising the Department. This seemed to weaken the BR position or, at the best, it seemed to make them nervous about reaching a decision with us. We were, after all, dealing with a perfectly normal business situation but, as will be seen, somehow the BR position was constantly hampered and undermined by having to look over their shoulders. It would have been so much easier if we in BTH could have felt the strength of the support of Morgan Grenfell in the efforts to achieve what their clients, BR, had stated as their objective but this was never the case.

On 13th August, I met with Mr. Bosworth in his role as Chairman of British Rail Investments Limited to assess the position. I was handed the formal letter of rejection which included an objective to see if we could together work out how we could move towards agreement. A matter that was causing the Secretary of State great concern was how he could justify a negotiated price before Parliament. It was believed, indeed stated as being known, that a large number of groups within the private sector had expressed interest in the hotels. We were quite confident that was not the position since we were in very close touch with everyone who was anyone in the hotel world. We knew there were some property speculators and one or two interested parties whose aim would be to acquire, operate for a short time and dispose of the properties. Over the years, people had written to various people in the Department and in BR and the kind of letters were usually of the type which said they were hoping they would be kept informed should any decision be taken to dispose; letters far removed from becoming the basis of a negotiation. There were probably approaching 100 such letters on various files and it was decided that Morgan Grenfell would be used to analyse this dossier in an attempt to overcome the Department's pressure to test the market. The fact was, there had been no other serious offer other than that put forward by the buyout team. The BR Board supported by Trade Unions were anxious to obtain the benefits of a smooth, orderly and quick transfer of ownership. From whatever angle they looked at the evidence, it could not be interpreted to support the view of the Department that the real problem was to get all the buyers in an orderly queue.

We had a long discussion on the best way of handling our normal staff communications problems. People are, in these circumstances, entitled to some knowledge about what is going on so far as it can affect their future livelihoods. The BR objective was clear and Mike Bosworth was extremely anxious to put the BR objective to the staff but I was not in favour of him doing so. I believed it better to hold back until there was something quite conclusive for him to announce. I was convinced that the staff knew what BR wanted to do since I had told them. We concluded it better for the managers to be given a complete exposition on what had happened so far so that they could speak to their staff with authority and knowledge. In addition, we decided to send a letter to every member of staff broadly indicating what had happened so far and how we were now hoping to proceed to a conclusion. Communication to the staff was essential and it was impossible to make bureaucrats understand that these people wanted to know what was to happen, that they were asking every day, but it was particularly difficult to make them understand that the workpeople were entitled to know without being labelled as a union sympathiser.

In order to avoid seeking permission of the Secretary of State for the sale, the first proposal excluded equity ownership by BR so that when the Chairman of BR told the Secretary of State of this privatisation plan for BTH, he could excuse himself for any responsibility on the prices obtained as had been done at the time of the Gleneagles deal. He could pass the entire responsibility to the Chairman of BR and avoid any flak in the Commons. At the worst, he would survive politically even if Sir Peter Parker had to be beaten about the head. But, of course, the rules changed and what was no more than a courtesy to explain what BR had decided, suddenly became a total involvement by the Politicians and Bureaucrats. The very thought of letting the BR Chairman make a decision of this magnitude had become far too risky! The Chairman, the BR Board, the BRIL Board, the BTH Board were all missing the vial point in their commercial judgement and omitting to note the importance of the Political ideology – they were behaving like businessmen and that might be a problem. One thing was certain and that was, there was a complete change in the rules. We had turned up to play Soccer and since we looked the stronger side they decided we had to play with a Rugby ball whose bounce would be more in keeping with their approach.

A check by our advisers brought only limited qualification to the acceptability of BR being involved. This was mainly because other potential investors were cautious about the likelihood of the long term holding of shares of BR. A political whim which directed their sale could obviously have detrimental effects on the remainder of the investors.

On 19th August, there was a meeting between principals and advisers on both sides. The meeting was split into two quite distinct parts, one of which was led by Morgan Grenfell and the other by Mike Bosworth. The Morgan Grenfell part was concerned with the wish to promote a sale by tender and seeing if the tender in its terms could be varied to enable the buyout team to participate. Kleinwort Benson held the line they had

141

always advised that to participate in a tender was practically impossible.

The reasoning behind this was purely concerned with the financing of our proposal. Relative to the total involved, my two colleagues and I had little cash to contribute. There was no doubt that we could get people to support us in a negotiated deal but not to agree to put up money to enable us to enter a bid against others. If you win in a tender, you have paid more than anyone else was willing to pay and that is not seen as good business. All of the argument would not sway Morgan Grenfell's view that it was possible for us to proceed along the tender route. Of course, they had the advantage that they were not advising us and, if subsequently they were wrong, it didn't matter. We succeeded in stopping any further progress on the work concerned with the tender until we had completed the discussions requested by the Secretary of State.

For the second half of the discussion, Mike Bosworth took the lead and this became concerned with how we could succeed. We were encouraged by being asked to presume that we would be allowed to have the management contracts for both the Great Eastern and the Great Northern Hotels and given the freedom to suggest different ways of BR participating in the new company.

Much encouraged by this positive thinking, a week of pretty hectic work began. We continued to have the great support that was needed from Sir Alexander Glen and from James Forbes. Ideas abounded from the management team and by the 26th August I was able to discuss several evaluated ideas with Mike Bosworth. This contact was imperative in order that the great amount of common ground that existed between parent and subsidiary could be properly explored and developed. It wasn't a question of trying to fix something since the whole of any proposal had got to be approved by the BRIL Board and the BR Board, but a common sense way of avoiding the unnecessary work of chasing hares that had no chance of succeeding when presented to either of those senior bodies.

The communication with the staff and managers brought very quick response and something approaching 50% of the total staff had indicated a wish to be involved in share ownership.

It was also clear that BR and BRIL had appreciated the vast expense that could be avoided if they did not have to follow the tender route; property agents fees for tender documentation; legal fees and fees to merchant bankers were accepted as making serious inroads into any money obtained from a sale by that method route. Additionally, account was being taken of the increasing value to the shareholders of an equity holding in a company that had done all the hard work to set itself onto a profitable road. The current profit performances were reflecting the turn round that had to be achieved. All these financial advantages were crystal clear before considering the imponderable value of risking industrial relations deterioration.

By 27th August, a path was emerging and one that as a general direction would be acceptable as a business deal by BR and BRIL. BR did not want to be left with a few hotels which they would have difficulty operating until they could be disposed of. It was therefore seen as sensible for the buyout team to take all of the hotels, placing no constraints upon their undertaking the immediate sale of the less profitable. Unlike the Gleneagles arrangements, BR would not insist upon participation on any profits on the sale of those hotels within a short period of time. To help the buyout team over immediate short term cash flow problems, it was agreed that the Great Eastern and the Great Northern could be the subject of management contracts. This was sensible from a BR point of view in the light of the increased value of these two sites on completion of development plans envisaged at each location.

Together with our advisers, we worked up some six different options, all in the general direction that we had agreed. It was our hope that Morgan Grenfell and Kleinwort Benson could guide us onto the more detailed evaluation of the most acceptable options. Those hopes began to founder when it became clear that the valuation made some six months earlier was that upon which the politicians and bureaucrats were placing so much importance. A valuation is not the precise thing that politicians would have liked it to be but they saw this as a tablet of stone against which any commercial deal had to be defended. The only solution they could see was some form of auction in which everyone had an equal chance. One sensed that the valuation was being treated as an alternative offer that was on the table. Christie/Druce were challenged to put more precise reasoning behind their futures. Morgan Grenfell were in no position to express a view directly on the Christie figures. There was no way we could help in this dilemma. To a large extent, we were not really very interested in Christie's valuation. Our concern was to pay sufficient for the assets that would enable us to produce an adequate return for investors in our Company. We could see that the Politicians and Bureaucrats were more concerned with establishing a base they could defend and they could not be moved from thinking that the valuation was a certain offer with a further queue of people waiting to top it.

In a very short time, the matter was becoming almost desperate. A business deal was seen as quite possible by BR, BRIL and BTH but it was now being thwarted because it was capable of being attacked in a Political arena. This, of course, in hindsight is particularly sickening when, some six months later, we were to learn that the valuation had actually been reduced by £3 million because of the terms of the tender documents. That, in itself, made absolute nonsense of what was going on in the first two weeks of September 1982. The matter was finally brought to a head by Sir Peter Parker calling a meeting at the only time that was possible, namely over breakfast on 16th September with Peter (now Sir Peter) Lazarus, who was the senior civil servant responsible for this work. This meeting was conducted on the basis that we were not doing some book exercise or case study but there was a matter concerning a real business and real people that, by now, was being greatly influenced by rumours, leaks and speculation, the origin of which we knew was not us.

A number of senior staff were voting with their feet and there was absolutely no way that we could engage people to replace three General Managers of hotels and the President of the Company in America who had all resigned unless what was going to happen to the Company was very clear. It was also made clear that if a tender route was followed, it would almost certainly mean the breaking up of the group which had been said to be politically important to preserve, and the very delicate British Rail industrial relations problems could be at risk.

The meeting was left in no doubt that time was of the essence and that if we were not very careful, we would have nothing to sell as a going concern.

The meeting was essential but, of course, it was also extremely dangerous because we were forcing bureaucrats into making a decision and to repeat the warning that Mike Bosworth had constantly given to do so was to run the severe risk of getting a negative answer. At that stage, it was difficult to avoid being thoroughly disenchanted with the public sector set up. I was Chief Executive of a business. I held my Board in high esteem just as I did the more senior Boards of BRIL and BR. The size of the business problem with which they had to deal was well within their ability and, so far as BR was concerned, represented a very small part of their total command. Yet, they were interrupted at every turn by a Political/Bureaucratic machine who successfully concealed any business ability they might have. No small wonder we so strongly supported the privatisation philosophy.

Because the matter of valuation was so important, we decided to change our tack and make a bid for fewer hotels. The reason for this was that by selling those units where we were most confident in the profit projections, we were able to get much closer to the individual evaluations that had been made. On 29th September, on our behalf, Kleinwort Benson Limited made a formal offer to purchase ten units and take management contracts on a further two. During the course of the discussions on valuation we had formed the view that there was common ground in that Christie/Druce had been influenced in their valuation by their opinion of the profit potential. Being willing to disclose to them, our opinion of the potential, and they were doing likewise, we were able to identify the areas where we were taking similar views and those were we were clearly some way apart. In formulating these revised proposals, we felt that we had substantially dealt with all the points that Morgan Grenfell were raising as areas of difficulty.

The proposal offered £20.5 million for the following:-

1. Freehold: Midland Hotel, Manchester, Turnberry Hotel, Turnberry. Royal Station Hotel, York. Welcombe Hotel, Stratford-on-Avon. Manor House Hotel, Moretonhampstead.

Tregenna Castle Hotel, St Ives.   Lochalsh Hotel, Kyle of Lochalsh.

2. Long Lease: Grosvenor Hotel, London – 125 years

3. Short Lease: Charing Cross Hotel, London – 20 years. Great Northern Hotel, London – 10 years

4. Ten Years Management Contracts: Great Eastern Hotel, London. Central Hotel, Glasgow.

We had been led to believe that valuation of all the hotels was £38.5 million. The valuation of the hotels for which we were not bidding was £15 million. Our proposal, together with the confidence of their own advisers in obtaining the valuations for the remainder of the hotels, would result in BR receiving £35.5 million gross for the 21 hotels comprising the BTH group. It is pertinent, yet again, to remember that the revision in valuation was not disclosed. In our offer, we were able to confirm participation and that, in order to achieve this, we were proposing to reserve 10% of the equity for the staff to purchase. Our proposals included the deferring of the payment of £6 million over four years. This was necessary because of the cash flow problems that the new company would have.   When discounted to the net present value, the discount on valuation was about the same as the professional expenses in disposal that would be incurred by selling by tender.   In other words, we matched the valuation.

Things moved very quickly.   There were a number of changes of a relatively minor nature but all aimed at closing the gap between the two negotiating parties.   There was quite a bit of changing position by BR as to whether they were prepared to take equity or not.   We continued to welcome a BR participation since, over the years, we had built up a number of very useful marketing and selling relationships with BR that were unique to us and   we were very anxious not to lose these.   We were overjoyed when a message came from the BRIL Board Meeting of 5th October 1982 indicating that our proposal had their approval.   That was a very important step for us to have achieved and the point at which, with our advisers, we moved forward to the next exciting stage of actually raising the money. We had enjoyed the experience we'd had with British Linen Bank in raising funds in the Gleneagles project and we were, of course, recalling that we were then given three months in which to convince potential investors, show them the assets and put the whole of that financial deal together. James Capel were the stockbrokers selected by Kleinwort Benson to look after the next stage.

I drafted the format on which the management contracts should be based and set up our team to progress with the matter before moving to take a few days' holiday to the north of Inverness. I left on 15th October taking with me a copy of the Guardian which carried a well informed story that the Secretary of State had decided to reject the latest submission. My wife and I managed to have three enjoyable days before arriving at Thurso on the afternoon of Tuesday 19th October, when telephone calls from our advisers required me back in London to make a presentation to potential investors on Wednesday 20th October. Whilst everyone subsequently denied it, Kleinwort Benson had been told that an offer very close to that we had made would be accepted, provided we could go firm on it by 21st October. The whole thing seemed too ridiculous for words and, naturally, we were suspicious that we were being set up – three months to set up the Gleneagles finance and forty eight hours to set up this one. However, in the event, I got back to London and together with John Tee and Derek Plant, put on a presentation. We were amazed at the number of people who turned up at such short notice to hear it. There was a genuine interest but nervousness that people would have at being given such short notice. In the event, people could not commit themselves against the timescale set down.

I have nothing but praise for the speed with which James Capel and Company got people together and for the tremendous support that they gave us in making our presentation. It was clear from that wasted effort that, just as had been the case with the Gleneagles project, people needed to be carefully handled and individually met to build up their confidence in the investment and the management. We could not get commitment within the 48 hours or so we had been given. It was quite unreasonable to require it and it was no surprise, in our investigation that followed, to be unable to find who was responsible for setting us up to try.

Together with our advisers, we were beginning to feel quite helpless. We reached agreement with our principals and it was clear that something outside our control was causing problems. There was a meeting on 27th October between Mike Bosworth and the Secretary of State, David Howell, at which the confusion that was being created by departmental indecision was laid firmly on the line. There were some exceedingly delicate IR problems being discussed in BR with the Trade Unions but Trade Union support for the BTH Board proposals seemed detrimental. It seemed that actually to achieve something with Trade Union support did not collect brownie points for progressing a political career at that time. What we could really have done with was the Trade Unions saying they would call the railway out on strike if we decided to proceed with the buyout. We could then have been seen to be taking on the Unions on a Management must manage basis, be good chaps in the eyes of Government to be supported.

A key Trade Union consultation meeting had been arranged for the afternoon of Wednesday 27th October, after which I was to meet Mike Bosworth on the 6 o'clock train to Manchester. I was fairly depressed because I thought he was going to tell them that the consortium buyout was not to go ahead at all. In the event, and to my absolute delight, he told the Trade Unions that we were going to proceed and, on 28th, all managers were informed at a Management Conference in the Midland Hotel that our proposal, submitted on 5th October, had been accepted and we would be proceeding.

I was immediately in touch with Kleinwort Benson and all the professional advisers, lawyers (Stephenson Harwood) accountants (Peat Marwick & Mitchel) and stockbrokers (James Capel) were asked to assemble their teams. Everything has come alive. Great excitement from the management abounded. We could have a company created before the remainder of the hotels were put up for sale and thus be in a strong position to bid for any of those units.

On Friday 29th October, there was a particularly difficult meeting with the civil servants who now seemed to be getting a little too close for comfort to Morgan Grenfell. Managerially, Mr. Bosworth was in the driving seat, acting on behalf of the

Chairman of the British Railways Board. It was for him to defend the BR decision against an examination by civil servants. Morgan Grenfell were present. Also at the meeting was James Urquart who, in addition to being a member of the British Rail Investments Limited Board, was, following the illness of Cliff Rose, in charge of the negotiations with the Trade Unions. Sir Peter Baldwin, the permanent secretary, who led for the civil servants, was not at all comfortable in accepting there was pressure from the Trade Unions to support the British Rail Board's decision.

The position was slowly grinding to the dangerous one of forcing a decision and constantly I recalled Mike Bosworth's earlier predictions in those circumstances. Civil servants had got to face the position where their files would have to be marked to show that any decision they had to recommend to the Minister could be seen to be that of the British Railways Board. The Board were not clobbering the Trade Unions hard enough to suit everyone. Here was a decision that had the support of a Trade Union who, rightly or wrongly, were making a bit of a fuss about rostering of crews. The deal agreed for BTH, like every deal, did not receive an unqualified seal of perfection from the financial advisers to the Railways Board who seemed to be close to the Department. There was no decision taken at the meeting and it ended with the civil servants wondering how they could test the proposed offer against an offer that someone else might be prepared to make if someone could be found who was interested in a similar package.

This was slowly driving every one of us involved to despair. The discussions had got nothing whatsoever to do with the good business practice or satisfactory development of the country's investments. We were all being expected to work for the comfort of politicians and the protection of official files.

Sit Peter Parker and my Deputy Chairman, Sir Alexander Glen were in touch late on the Sunday evening. Sir Peter confirmed his strong support for the decision that he had taken and expressed the view at the Board Meeting that was to take place the following Thursday, 4th November, that there would be no letting go by BR and he proposed taking the decision for reconfirmation to the BR Board on the basis that the gap between the opinion of Morgan Grenfell and the price offered was so small as to be trivial and that BRIL had, in fact, for no other serious offers. An appointment brief was to be prepared for the Chairman.

Advice subsequently received suggested that a memorandum be submitted to the Board Meeting and this was done. We started the paper by dealing very briefly with the history. The management team of BTH, supported by Kleinwort Benson, had submitted their proposals for a consortium buyout of 18 hotels on 15th June for completion on 31st October. These proposals had been partially supported by BRIL who required the BR Board to make the judgement on the amount of discount below valuation that could be allowed to reflect cost savings that would accrue to BR and the benefits that would be derived from a development that had Trade Union support. In other words, a value judgment on matters that could not be justified or evaluated by financial criteria. The Secretary of State, in August, had urged the Board not to support the proposals. Subsequently, BRIL, Morgan Grenfell, Kleinwort Benson and the management team co-operated to produce the consortium's revised proposal for 12 hotels, leaving 11 to be sold by the public tender route. The revised proposal had been approved by BRIL on 5th October and by the BR Board at its last meeting on 7th October.

The Secretary of State had not been disposed to support the Board's decision because Morgan Grenfell were not, from a strict financial standpoint, able to support a discount that was seen as £3.6 million, being the difference between the Christie/Druce valuation of £24.1 million and the consortium's offer of £20.5 million. Morgan Grenfell had verbally expressed the view that from the financial viewpoint, a discount of £2 million may be justified. Morgan Grenfell never became involved in making judgements on the effects on operational aspects of BR. It is again, here, most important to remember that the valuation upon which everyone was basing comments was claimed at the meeting on March 1st to have been overstated by £3 million because of the terms that were being imposed. After adjusting the valuation or a proportion of that £3 million, the discount was, in fact, little more than the £2 million which was said to be acceptable.

The British Railways Board were informed of the view of BTH that the discount could be justified by direct cash benefits to BR plus a number of benefits requiring more qualitative judgement.

The direct cash benefits were seen to emerge from not having to pay redundancy payments to between 30 and 35 staff that would be taken into the consortium from Headquarters; that cash of £15 million would be received two to three months earlier than proceeding on a tender route; that similar commissions or fees to merchant banks and lawyers would also be avoided and that the customary trading losses that the Company incurred in the early part of each calendar year would accrue to the new owners. These direct cash benefits evaluate to be of the order of £1.5 million.

We left for qualitative judgement, the problem of continuing to manage a crumbling organisation under notice for sale where key people in the hotels would continue to leave a company at the then disturbing and surely increasing rate; that service and quality would consequently deteriorate and that the longer term bookings of corporate and conference organisers would bypass the company. Finally, as a qualitative judgement, we asked the Board to consider the value in achieving the objective of keeping a large, important hotel company together.

The options available to BR Board were summarised as follows:-

1.   To sell all the hotels by public tender.

2.   To confirm the decision they had taken on 7th October and seek approval of the Secretary of State.

3.   To amend the decision taken on 7th October by eliminating equity participation of BR which would, in turn, eliminate the need to seek the approval of the Secretary of State on the precedent set by his predecessor in dealing with the Gleneagles project.

The Board were urged to adopt Option 3 and thus, at a stroke, eliminate political involvement

I had a call at lunchtime on 2nd November from Mike Bosworth which was not encouraging. So far as he could judge, he was not making any progress. The worst news was that he learned that the letter to turn down the proposal was, in fact, drafted but the Department were refraining from sending in until after the BR Board Meeting on the 4th, presumably hoping BR would reverse their earliest decision. We were keeping very close contact with Kleinwort Benson and both they and we were seeking any opportunity we could find to meet and continue some negotiations. Negotiation in any conventional sense was completely impossible between merchant banks because we could not understand Morgan Grenfell's position, so rarely did they seem to be working for BR. So far as we were able to see, we were meeting every obstacle that they could identify to us but we never could get clarity of what was acceptable.

During this time, my mind frequently returned to that conversation I had had with Peter Thompson at the RAF Club in October when he said that the biggest problem they had in setting up the NFC arrangements was getting the Department and the Politicians to say what they saw as an acceptable price on which they would negotiate a deal. We were completely locked in that position. We had agreed with the British Railways Board; we had agreed with BRIL; we were poised with our advisers to set up the funds to complete the deal and nowhere could we have conversation to take the matter to a conclusion.

I was not privileged to be at the BR Board Meeting of 4th November. My mind was not altogether on the subjects that I had gone to discuss at the University of Bath and I had arranged to stop on my journey from Bath to Sheffield at the Welcombe Hotel to see if my contact on the Board had any information. I arrived at the Welcombe Hotel at about 4.30p.m. where the message was to speak to one of the Board Members.

At last, it seemed that we were going to stand up and be counted and show who was running the business. I was told that the Board spent an hour and a half discussing how they were to handle the Department and that there was only one Member who was opposed to a straight confrontation with the Secretary of State. The Board decided that the Chairman was to see the Secretary of State and require him either to withdraw his interference with their decision or make a formal direction as to the course they were to take. The alternative was that the Board would go public and explain the extent to which they had been leaned on by the Politicians. A meeting was duly arranged with the Secretary of State.

Over the weekend, Mike Bosworth rang to let me know what had happened and see what next steps could be taken to brief him for a meeting that had been set up with Morgan Grenfell and the Department for Tuesday 9th November.

The meeting with the Secretary of State achieved nothing; the only hope was that it might had gained some time but; out of it, came a whole new series of ball games which wanted us to go ahead with the tender programme but put together as one package the hotels for which the consortium had made an offer.

If then the offer stood up against any others that came in on the tender, he would allow the Buyout to proceed. On Monday 8th November, we met with Kleinwort Benson who were able to reaffirm their support provided the package as we had put it together was accepted, the price agreed and the rules of play agreed by the Secretary of State. All we wanted was formal agreement on a business deal and then to be allowed to implement it. But, of course, it did actually require a decision from Politicians and their Bureaucrats and one from which they could not escape and on which they stood close to defend themselves.

The meeting with the Department and Morgan Grenfell took place fairly early on 9th November and, to my horror, by 09.45, Mr. Bosworth was on the telephone to say that they had not got on very well. John Palmer was the senior civil servant present. In typical "Yes Minister" language, it was explained that the Secretary of State was taking the view that no more time should be given to the project and that enough time had now been spent. Most of the discussion was concentrated on how a tender document could be constructed with one of the lots being the same as the submission that we had made. There was absolutely no progress made in either getting the rules laid down or an indication of an acceptable price.

This called for great personal control. Throughout the whole of this prolonged tedious business, the BTH Board or those of us who represented it, had never fallen out with the Chairman or

Deputy Chairman of BR because we were quite convinced that a good business deal had been done between us. If anything, we were too sympathetic to the problem they were trying to solve which was all to do with politics and nothing to do with business. I note that what I had said in the telephone conversation after the very disappointing meeting, was that I expected our lords and masters to tell the Minister that we expected a reply that said what was acceptable and stop procrastinating about how, what might subsequently be agreed, could be defended. There comes a time to stand up and be counted even though careers, political or otherwise, are at stake. I can only conclude as I read my notes sometime later that perhaps I was just a little upset by John Palmer telling them that the Secretary of State had taken the view that enough time had been given. So far as we were concerned, they had failed to give any reasonable time to the business aspects and never had they given an indication of what they would find acceptable.

On 11th November, all resistance in the BR Board must have collapsed when I received the formal letter saying that the offer of 5th October could not be accepted.

Mike Bosworth had the embarrassing task of writing to all the people who were at the conference three weeks earlier when he had indicated that the consortium buy-out proposals had been accepted. It must have been an extremely difficult letter for him to write. I always felt that I was extremely close to him during the time he was wrestling with the political problem and, perhaps it was at that time more than any other, I realised that personally I was totally unsuited to head up a public sector business because there is no way that I could have extended the courtesy to the Politicians and Bureaucrats that was extended by either Sir Peter Parker or Mike Bosworth.

Even though the BR Board had been comprehensively defeated, or they had unconditionally surrendered to the establishment, they did continue to encourage us in our efforts to put together a response to the tender invitation.

CHAPTER EIGHTEEN – THE TENDER

None of us could pretend, at the time or with the benefit of hindsight, that we were not knocked completely for six by the decision of Government that they would not negotiate a deal. But we had to pick ourselves up and at least had the consolation of knowing that we had reached an end of the hopelessness of trying to negotiate with a sponge. The Establishment had won. They would not indicate what they wanted by way of a deal and we could only conclude that they did not know as they had proved to be so unwilling to negotiate in a normal business sense. The management was still absolutely convinced that the right course was to fight to the very end for the principle of keeping the Company, or a large portion of it, together. The great tradition, history and quality of BTH in the hotel industry of the world was worth fighting to the death.

We were utterly convinced that, if we did not do that then there was the real risk that the splendid British properties would fall into the hands of people who, in the main were little more than property speculators because we knew who had been 'sniffing around' them. There was, indeed, concern expressed in Parliament on 20th December when Mr. Booth asked if the Secretary of State would direct that the British Railways Board would not sell any British Transport Hotels to foreign buyers. Mr. Howell replied that he knew no reason why such a restriction should be considered. Perhaps it was a pity that the Secretary of State did not take a little more note of the people who knew perfectly well that there was not the queue of hoteliers waiting to buy these fine hotels.

In spite of the fact that Kleinwort Benson had, at the beginning of this trail, placed on record their view that it would not be possible to put together a bid if a tender route were selected, they nevertheless stood firmly by us and together with our advisers, James Capel, Stephenson and Peat, Marwick Mitchell, they helped the management team brace themselves for the enormous strain they were to be put under up till the middle of February when the tender had to be submitted.

We could, by now, see that the Company had been completely turned round and that all the measures that we had taken to produce a profitable company were paying off. It is adequate to quote the British Railways Board Report and Accounts for 1982 where the Chairman referring to the management and staff of BTH acknowledges that

"under formidable pressure, turned in an admirable performance converting losses at the hotel level in 1981 into a marginal profit."

We had also the benefit of having completed budgets for 1983 that enabled us to see the confidence expressed by managers on how much could be built on the turn round they had achieved. Unfortunately, to be really convincing to a City institution, we needed another year building up the profits, which, of course, is precisely the timing the BTH Board had advocated a year earlier and had been rejected by BRIL working to the directive to achieve disposal in the life of this Parliament. We had the product about right, we had a good management team and we were left with one problem. This was how to sort out a headquarters that was far too big. We knew exactly how we were going to do this but could not achieve many of the planned savings while tied to the requirements of British Railways accountancy and administration, much of which had to respond to the requirements placed upon them Treasury by methods.

The actual figure work of putting together the group for which we were prepared to tender, presented very little problem.

We had an excellent management accounting system that enabled us to review any part of our business quickly and simply. At the two extremes, were arguments as to whether it would be better to bid for, say, ten of the most profitable units. In which case it was more probable that the bid would meet more competition from other hoteliers who could make a good assessment of our best units. At the other end of the scale there was a strong argument to bid for the lot provided there were no constraints on subsequent disposal of the less profitable units. The strength for that case lay in our conviction that no-one would bid for the lot and a belief that BR would find a bid for the whole that was lower than the sum total of the bids for the parts, more attractive since, at a stroke, it dealt with their problem and particularly when it was from a purchaser against whom there could be no objection.

There was a real risk that a number of individual investors from overseas might appear. The political instability in some countries creates the need for homes for former leaders, or the provision of a bolt hole in power; situations which could make several of our establishments very attractive to foreign buyers of substantial wealth. The professional advisers wrestled with the problems. There was no outstanding financial advantage or disadvantage one way or the other. Sometimes, an easier cash flow problem was possible and other times, a better profit return was possible but the difference in every case was marginal and, in the end, the matter rested on the advice of James Capel as to the amount of money that could be raised. The final decision which everyone supported was in favour of going for the biggest group possible. We decided that only four hotels should be excluded from our bid. The Adelphi Hotel, Liverpool was excluded because we had been seeking permission to sell it anyway for two or more years and were convinced that without spending at least £1 million on it, it was unlikely that we would be able to match competition for the limited market in Liverpool. We excluded both hotels in Glasgow because of their poor business performances over the past two years and our view that this position was not likely to change. The Central Hotel had been a wonderful hotel in its day but we were quite convinced that its day had passed and that the complete conversion of the property to some other use was the best long term plan for that building which was so closely integrated with the railway station. The North British Hotel, a fine site, given a substantial capital investment ought to be capable of being developed. But capital of the level that we believed to be required could not be financed to the new company within a reasonable span of time. We had looked long and hard at the Great Northern Hotel, Peterborough, with a fine history of being the halfway meeting place for people travelling by rail from the North to meet their colleagues in the South. Our Peterborough experience had not been very good. Over the past years, little attempt had been made to change the hotel and new hotels provided an adequate room cover for our business needs. In our view, the bulk of visitors to Peterborough stayed elsewhere.

We also included in our bid, the management contracts for the Great Eastern Hotel and the Great Northern Hotel to make a group of 19 hotels with about 2,500 rooms, approaching £30 million turnover and just under 2,000 staff.

The executive directors formed a company, Concorde Hotels plc, for the purpose of responding to the tender. Concorde proposed to tender £35 million for the 17 hotels plus the two management contracts. They proposed that £27 million should be payable in cash on completion and that £8 million would be paid in four equal instalments of £2 million at the end of year one and subsequent three years.

The capital of Concorde was to consist of ordinary shares of £1 each and a 5 – 16.5% stepped interest first mortgage debenture stock. The debenture stock was to be secured by a first charge on the freehold and leasehold assets of the company and repayable at par 31st December 2008. The stepped interest would give a gross redemption yield of 131/2%. James Capel saw this as a well constructed proposition and were confident that they could raise the finance on that basis if only we could put an agreed deal to the market. Hanging over the whole arrangements was the fact that this was the first time ever that they had attempted to raise money to back a bid against an open tender. There was no doubt at all in their minds that had they been backing a negotiated deal, the proposals they were putting to the market would have been snapped up.

BR, in the circumstances were doing all they could. Against a background of pressure from Government to meet its Political ends by disposal of its subsidiary businesses and unfortunately, against greater pressure from Government to meet its financial objectives in spite of heavy losses through industrial action.

BR agreed that if full subscription of the placing were not possible, that it, or one of its subsidiaries, would subscribe for 20% of the capital.

On this basis, a full placing memorandum was prepared and discussions were held with several finance houses. Meetings of groups of potential investors were held in London and Edinburgh, visits were arranged and a thorough professional job was done by all the parties involved in endeavouring to launch Concorde Hotels plc as a successor to British Transport Hotels Limited.

No matter how good the professional advisers are, they must have appropriate time in this kind of exercise (apoint adequately proved in the Gleneagles exercise). In all, we made our presentation to fifty institutions at three meetings. The response to the tender was required on 14th February. We held our meetings with potential investors on 7th and 9th February. Time between discussion and response was short, no follow up was possible. It was completely impossible to risk holding meetings any earlier because, effectively, it would have meant a public disclosure of our bid to the people against whom we were bidding. Because of the nature of financing our proposals, the details of our bid were at grave risk of becoming public information and certainly any competing bidder could find out about our proposals with ease by posing as a potential investor.

There is an interesting letter from Christie & Co. dated 30th November 1982 to the Deputy Chairman of British Railways Board saying that during the period of negotiations prior to the announcement of the tender, they accepted my right to state our case but that any continued commentary "is proving damaging to the outcome of the sale" and that

"it is clearly not proper or desirable that we as agents should be drawn into a debate as to the political wisdom of a sale to the management, we write to request that the management of BTH are dissuaded from making any further public statement until our marketing has been completed in February 1983".

Meanwhile, they were pleased to advise their principals that since the launch, enquiries were coming in "at the rate of fifty a day, which we find most encouraging". A point well noted by those anxiously waiting for a fleet of mail vans to draw up with the tenders on 14th February.

For fear of the information being used by our competitors, we dare not let it be known exactly what we were prepared to bid for, yet here were the selling agents asking my Chairman to lean on me to stop me endeavouring to get opinion on our side as the cause they should support.

Handling the launch of the prospectus was a pretty full managerial task. We had still got the Company to run because it was in no-one's interest for us to let it fail. We were seriously trying to buy out and even if we were to fail, there were the futures of many people to consider and those futures would depend upon their managerial track record. We were also building up many contacts with other organisations who were anxious to be involved with Concorde Hotels in the future development of the Company. Arnold Palmer, Buckley Development Company were anxious to join with us in the development of Turnberry. An insurance company were talking with us about financing the development of the Midland Hotel, Manchester, in conjunction with the development of the old Central Station. A South African Company were interested in the possibility of a joint development of the Great Western Royal and the Reo Stakis organisation would have been welcome bedfellows for a strong association in many of the hotels. The potential future development was most exciting.

However, it was not to be. The fears which had been expressed on 14th June that the tender route could not be followed by the management team proved to be right. As we assessed the position on the morning of 14th February, we had support for only half the amount that we need and very sadly had to abandon our buy out hopes. The advice to ourselves and the British Railways Board by Kleinwort Benson in June 1982 proved to be right. Those advising the Secretary of State and the British Railways Board that it was possible to pursue a management buyout through an open tender route were wrong but, of course, they drew strength of their confidence that the Secretary of State would have an enormous response to his initiative of selling by tender.

Being convinced that the result of the tender would result in the annihilation of British Transport Hotels, I decided on 18th February to have one final throw to save the Company in its entirety. In the tender proposals BR reserved the right to reject any offer. If they really did mean that they wanted to keep the Company together, they had the power to reject the responses if no successor to BTH emerged from the tender. If the politicians really did hope that the group could be kept together, as they expressed, then there was no reason why, if the tender responses were poor, BR should themselves not proceed on the lines of the proposals made by Concorde Hotels plc. Effectively, all this meant was to accept the BTH Board proposals and use the new Concorde company as the vehicle. It could easily be demonstrated that, provided the Company were given the freedom that it proposed in its placing document and followed the proposals in that document which were little different from the BTH Business Strategy submitted in 1981 and the revised financial structure agreed by BR in 1980, that, by the end of 1985, the Company could be floated and BR would obtain a net present value of something of the order of £40 million. Apart from a minor flutter on the afternoon of 21st February, when further copies of the placing document were requested, nothing further was heard.

To say that the results of the tender caused some surprise is a masterpiece of understatement. After all the build up and opinion expressed in radio interviews by the agents of expectations of the order of £50 million realisation, the letter of 30th November which suggested that my efforts were having a devastating effect on the marketing, and that enquiries were flooding in at the rate of 50 per day, it must have been a dreadful shock when, on 14th February, there was only 14 envelopes to open. There was not a single acceptable bid for the entire Group. There was not a single acceptable bid for more than eight. Three London hotels were sold to MF North plc, a company who owned one hotel in London and several small ones on the South coast; five were sold to Batchshire Limited who were part of Seaco Holdings Limited who owned one hotel in America and two in Europe. The hotel in Hartlepool was sold to West Hartlepool Steam Navigation Company Limited and the Adelphi was sold to Brittania Hotels Limited who had two other establishments. Eleven hotels remained unsold. Hardly a swoop by the leading hotel groups. The buyers from the tender process had barely a dozen establishments amongst them.

It was decided that the 11 remaining hotels would be the subject of a negotiated sale and, since there was only one organisation, the Virani Group, expressing any interest, the scope for negotiation was somewhat limited. The result of those negotiations was that, for £4.6 million, the Virani Group purchased eight hotels for an average room price of less than £6,000 and that included such hotels as the Manor House, Moretonhampstead; the Glasgow Central and the Royal Station Hotel, Hull. After all we had been through, trying to negotiate, at the end of the whole process there had to be a negotiated deal done and our Ugandan friends were alone in the field.

We had already made arrangements by which, in the event of the company not being held together as a single unit, my two colleagues, John Tee and Derek Plant would be given the opportunity of forming a company to run the Great Eastern and Great Northern Hotels on a short lease basis. The terms of those leases had already been agreed as part of the Concorde Hotels plc negotiations and it was a relatively simple procedure to make a slight change of direction and take appropriate steps to protect the security of my two colleagues.

On 1st March, I was invited to attend a meeting of British Rail Investment Limited which was to review the outcome of the tender. It is worth recalling that, throughout the whole of the battles we had fought, we had constantly been hammered about a valuation that had been made by the professional advisers because that was a base from which the Secretary of State could defend any decision in the House. The meeting was not at all relaxed and I don't suppose my presence in the room helped I dare say, the advisers of BRIL knew that I would not, if my circumstances so dictated, be adverse to pointing out to them their confidence in a realisation of £50 million and their assurance that my advisers were completely wrong in saying that the management team could not raise finance in a tender procedure. They did the best they could to defend what had been achieved. But how I kept my seat, I do not know, when one of the valuers went to great lengths to remind the meeting that he had changed his valuation downwards by £3 million some months ago because of property constraints and personnel terms that BR had insisted upon including. I did quietly wonder if the BR Board Executive on 22nd July knew, as it noted that the consortium could not proceed with a bid through the tender and that

"BRIL believed that a discount of 5% on the valuation was a reasonable reflection of the value of the elimination of such uncertainties which the tender option would incur; this excluded any benefits derived from the possible removal of IR uncertainties. A total discount of £4.5 million might therefore be justified".

At that time, I believed and I think BR Board Executive believed, that the valuation of the property included in the consortium buy out was £35 million. They were looking at that against an offer of £29 million which, subject to the terms of payment, had a present value of £27 million. Had they known that the real valuation was not £35 million but only £32 million they would have seen that allowing for their discount of £4.5 million justified for reasons of industrial relations certainty, speed of sale, avoidance of professional costs.etc., there was actually no gap at all between what was being offered and what they found acceptable.

We didn't hold a wake but set about doing our best to ensure that there was a smooth handover and, so far as the new owners were concerned, offering to do all we could to help them take over what we knew were extremely good businesses.

I think I was probably mentally exhausted and, not for the first time, Sir Alexander Glen, who was an incredible support to us throughout this time, took up the fight by writing to the Prime Minister on behalf of the British Transport Hotels Board to express deep concern at the outcome of public tender sale. Towards the end of 1982 when we were failing to make any inroads into the minds of the bureaucrats, Sir Alexander Glen had seen David Howell, the Secretary of State to try to make him understand the dangers of public tender. We had no wish to make our anxieties about what had happened the subject of the embarrassing political exploitation of him, particularly since, from the very beginning, we had all been in favour of privatisation. But, of course, our reasons for privatisation were quite different from those of the the politicians. We believed in it because it removed Bureaucrats and Politicians of either party from influencing the business so that decisions could be taken on the basis of commercial judgement and not as a matter of political expediency. The pressure not to sell Liverpool was a good example of that. Our views had been listened to sympathetically by British Railways Board. They had been understood and encouraged by Norman Fowler, the Secretary of State at the time of the Gleneagles deal, but subsequently, we were never allowed to put our views and have sensible discussion with either the Treasury or the Department. Morgan Grenfell with whom our advisers had many unsatisfactory discussions, were acting for BRIL, by whom they were employed, but they seemed to us to have direct contact with and speak for the Department. Sir Alexander pointed out to the Prime Minister that, given the relative freedom with which BTH set up Gleneagles Hotels plc in 1981, we were able to sell those hotels to the new company at £17,000 per bedroom despite the known requirement of £5 million of capital investment that had to be undertaken by the purchasers. The tender had produced only £14,000 per room for five prime location country hotels where little capital expenditure was required and it had directly resulted in the forced sale of a further eight hotels at a discount approaching 10% on valuation and for a room price of only £6,000. We had, as a Board, constantly expressed our concern at the professional costs to BRIL if they followed this tender route. We knew that, in the Gleneagles deal, the total cost (legal, selling, financial advice and accountancy) was less than 1 ½% of the sale's proceeds. Theoretically we were only able to guess the costs of the sale by tender and we would have taken a lot of convincing that it was less than £2 ½ million.

Sir Alexander expressed the concern of a great many people when he pointed out that BTH had accomplished privatisation constructively and commercially with three substantial deals in 1981 and 1982 and that the tender had annihilated an important company, where the Board, the management, the employees and the unions were all working together in the successful implementation of Government's initiatives and this was very regrettable from the Government's point of view.

The Prime Minister's reply on 30th March, naturally disagreed that the sale had produced an unsatisfactory outcome, saying that the Secretary of State for Transport and British Rail had agreed in 1981 on a policy for privatising the BTH Hotels as well as other non-rail subsidiaries as quickly as possible

"this would be to the benefit of the railways and the subsidiary concerned".

A very interesting point since in the Railways Board Report in 1982 they pointed out that much of the money realised had been needed to pay for the strikes and, since the subsidiary concerned was annihilated, it hardly received any benefit.

The Prime Minister went on to understand there were only two hotels to be disposed of and that early progress was expected. The fact was that the disposal of the remaining two took a further year or so. She felt that the final proceeds seemed likely to be close to the valuation given by BR's two firms of valuers, which

"as you know this is substantially more than the bids made by a consortium of institutions last summer, even when allowance is made for sale expenses and the difference in the timing of the sales".

Here, one can only assume that, like us, the writer of the Prime Minister's letter didn't know that the valuation had been reduced by £3 million. Mrs Thatcher concluded by noting the belief of the BTH Board that it could have privatised the hotels by 1985

"but BR have achieved a privatisation by early 1983 in a fashion offering a fair opportunity to all bidders including the existing management."

I think sufficient has been recorded to judge the fairness of the procedure to the existing management.

So far as a fair opportunity to other bidders is concerned, this must be acknowledged. In the case of Liverpool, the purchaser was immediately granted, by the Government, £1.3 million to invest in the hotel for which he paid the Government £900,000. So far as MF North were concerned, they subsequently sold within two years, the Grosvenor and the Great Western at substantial profits. Seaco sold Tregenna Castle and the Virani Group sold the Manor House Hotel, Moretonhampstead, within days of purchasing it. Indeed, a very fair opportunity for successful bidders!

Clearly, there was no future in endeavouring to continue correspondence at that level, and the Prime Minster was courteously thanked for her kind examination of the position.

As a matter of courtesy, Sir Alexander sent a copy of his letter to the Prime Minister to David Howell, the Secretary of State, whose reply again was concerned with the discount against valuation of management offers which is perfectly valid if you did not know that the valuation had been revised. A feature of the Secretary of State's reply was his anxiety to explain that the tender route that was subsequently adopted was

"by a decision of the Railways Board, not me".

The Secretary of State concluded by hoping that emphasis would be made on making

"the most of the opportunities that being in the private sector will bring to these distinguished hotels."

The conclusion was sad for everybody. The professional advisers of the Railways Board and the Department were left defending themselves, certainly not basking in any glory. The Secretary of State was sacked on 10th June and his minister was sacked on 13th June. The employees in the hotels certainly had not seen any great new dawn and, indeed, for many of them, the uncertainty of ownership has increased as the comings and goings of gentlemen of different nationality have traded the opportunities created for them by the Government.

Perhaps the depth of political understanding can be summarised in a letter that was addressed to the Managing Director of British Transport Hotels in August 1983, some four months after they had passed out of public ownership, complaining about the quality of the breakfast he had had in the Royal Station Hotel at York. The letter was from a Minister of the Crown.

ABOUT THE AUTHOR

Peter Land qualified as a Chartered Accountant in 1950 and immediately left the profession to quickly progress to be the Chief Account of British Rail, Western Railway in 1964. His potential in management was recognised and he became the youngest General Manager in 1968.

He formed National Carriers, to bring under one command the road transport activities of British Rail. He worked at the highest executive level from 1968 to 1983, frequently having to limit the damage to the business from the excess of Political ideology.

He was Managing Director of British Transport Hotels when, after a two year fight, he was ordered to sell the business as part of the privatisation policy of the Thatcher administration.

In retirement he became Chairman of a Health Authority and for twelve years had to fight in the same kind of war; Government of the day versus Civil Servants versus Treasury rules versus Business Management.

Printed in Great Britain
by Amazon